Windows® 7 Just the Steps™ FOR DUMMIES®

by Nancy Muir

WILEY

Wiley Publishing, Inc.

Windows® 7 Just the Steps™ For Dummies®

Published by
Wiley Publishing, Inc.
111 River Street
Hoboken, NJ 07030-5774
www.wiley.com

Copyright © 2009 by Wiley Publishing, Inc., Indianapolis, Indiana

Published by Wiley Publishing, Inc., Indianapolis, Indiana

Published simultaneously in Canada

For general information on our other products and services, please contact our Customer Care Department within the U.S. at 877-762-2974, outside the U.S. at 317-572-3993, or fax 317-572-4002.

For technical support, please visit www.wiley.com/techsupport.

Wiley also publishes its books in a variety of electronic formats. Some content that appears in print may not be available in electronic books.

Library of Congress Control Number: 2009932705

ISBN: 978-0-470-49981-8

Manufactured in the United States of America

10   9   8   7   6   5   4   3   2   1

About the Author

Nancy Muir is the author of over 50 books on technology and business topics. She has worked as a manager in both the publishing and software industries. Nancy holds a certificate in distance learning design and is the VP of Content and Curriculum for LOOKBOTHWAYS Foundation, an Internet safety company dedicated to developing free safety curriculums for children in grades K–12.

Dedication

To my fabulous husband, Earl Boysen, and my family and friends who make my tough deadlines and other writing stresses endurable.

Author's Acknowledgments

Thanks so much to all the folks at Wiley Publishing who make working with them such a pleasure, including acquisitions editor Kyle Looper, project editor Kim Darosett, copy editor Jen Riggs, and technical editor Lee Musick.

Publisher's Acknowledgments

We're proud of this book; please send us your comments through our online registration form located at http://dummies.custhelp.com. For other comments, please contact our Customer Care Department within the U.S. at 877-762-2974, outside the U.S. at 317-572-3993, or fax 317-572-4002.

Some of the people who helped bring this book to market include the following:

Acquisitions and Editorial

Project Editor: Kim Darosett

Acquisitions Editor: Kyle Looper

Copy Editor: Jen Riggs

Technical Editor: Lee Musick

Editorial Manager: Leah Cameron

Sr. Editorial Assistant: Cherie Case

Cartoons: Rich Tennant (www.the5thwave.com)

Composition Services

Project Coordinator: Katherine Crocker

Layout and Graphics: Claudia Bell, Ana Carrillo, Melanee Habig, Joyce Haughey, Andrea Hornberger, Melissa K. Jester, Christin Swinford

Proofreaders: Dwight Ramsey, Mildred Rosenzweig

Indexer: Johnna VanHoose Dinse

Publishing and Editorial for Technology Dummies

Richard Swadley, Vice President and Executive Group Publisher

Andy Cummings, Vice President and Publisher

Mary Bednarek, Executive Acquisitions Director

Mary C. Corder, Editorial Director

Publishing for Consumer Dummies

Diane Graves Steele, Vice President and Publisher

Composition Services

Debbie Stailey, Director of Composition Services

Contents at a Glance

I'm guessing you have a healthy dislike of computer books. You don't want to wade through a long tome on Windows 7. Rather, you just want to get in, find out how to do something, and get out. You're not alone. I was itching to write a book where I could get right to the details of how to do things — and move on. None of that telling you what I'm going to tell you, saying my piece, and then reviewing for you what I just said. That's why I was delighted to tackle a *Just the Steps For Dummies* book on Windows 7.

About This Book

Windows 7 is a very robust piece of software, with about as much functionality as Einstein on a good day. If you own a Windows 7 computer (and I assume you do, or you should rush back to the bookstore for a refund, pronto!), you're likely to spend a lot of time every day in the Windows 7 environment. Knowing how to harness the power of this operating system is what this book is all about. As the title suggests, I give you just the steps you need to do many of the most common Windows 7 tasks. This book is all about getting productive right away.

Why You Need This Book

You can't wait weeks to master Windows 7. It's where all your software lives as well as how you get to your e-mail and documents. You have to figure out Windows 7 quickly. You might need to poke around Windows and do work while learning. When you hit a bump in the road, you need a quick answer to get you moving again. This book is full of quick, clear steps that keep your learning in high gear.

▌▌▌▶ Introduction

Conventions used in this book

➡ When you have to type something in a text box, I put it in **bold** type.

➡ For menu commands, I use the ➪ symbol to separate menu items. For example, choose Tools➪Internet Options. The ➪ symbol is just my way of saying "Choose Internet Options from the Tools menu."

➡ Points of interest in some figures are circled. The text tells you what to look for, and the circle makes it easy to find.

 This icon points out insights or helpful suggestions related to tasks in the step list.

How This Book Is Organized

This book is conveniently divided into several handy parts.

Part I: Working in Windows 7

Here's where you get the basics of opening and closing software applications, working with files and folders to manage the documents you create, and using built-in Windows applications like the Calculator and WordPad. You also discover how to use the cool tools offered in Windows Gadget Gallery.

Part II: Getting on the Internet

The whole world is online, and you can't be left behind. Here's where I show you how to connect, how to browse using the newest version of Internet Explorer, ways for using the Internet to stay in touch when you're on the road, and how to do e-mail using Windows Live Mail.

Part III: Setting Up Hardware and Networks

In addition to software, Windows helps you work with hardware and connections between computers. You might have to make a little effort to set up new hardware or a home network. This part is where I show you how to do that, as well as how to make settings so displays and devices are easy to use and accessible if you have any vision, hearing, or other physical challenges.

Part IV: Customizing Windows

You can change a great deal about the appearance of the Windows desktop, including the background, colors, and a transparent effect called Windows Glass. In addition, you can

modify how features such as your mouse and keyboard work to help you if you have dexterity challenges, and set up the Windows Speech Recognition feature.

Part V: Using Security and Maintenance Features

Windows 7 provides lots of ways to keep your information safe, from passwords to protect your files to tools to prevent viruses and spyware from attacking your system. Several features also help keep your system up to date and trouble-free.

Part VI: Fixing Common Problems

Yes, I admit it, even Windows can have problems. Luckily, it also has tools to get you out of trouble. In this part, I explain how to deal with hardware and software problems as well as how to get help when you need it.

Part VII: Fun and Games

Finally, you've earned some fun. Go to these chapters to discover a world of games, music, photos, and video just waiting for you in Windows 7.

Get Ready To . . .

Whether you need to open a piece of software and get working, check your e-mail, or get online, just browse this book, pick a task, and jump in. Windows 7 can be your best friend if you know how to use it, and the tasks covered in this book will make you a Windows 7 master in no time.

Part I
Working in Windows 7

The 5th Wave   By Rich Tennant

UBER-USER DWAYNE GRANTZ CHALKS
UP BEFORE PUTTING WINDOWS 7
THROUGH ITS PACES.

Exploring the Windows 7 Desktop

*J*ust as your desk is the central area from which you do all kinds of work, the Windows 7 desktop is a command center for organizing your computer work. Here you find the Start menu, which you use to access information about your computer, files, folders, and applications. You'll also find a taskbar that offers settings, such as your computer's date and time, as well as shortcuts to your most frequently accessed programs or files.

In this chapter, you explore the desktop, which appears when you log on to Windows 7. Along the way, you discover the Recycle Bin, the area of the Windows 7 taskbar that lets you open frequently used programs, the notification area, and how to shut down your computer when you're done for the day.

Here, then, are the procedures that you can use to take advantage of the desktop features of Windows 7.

Get ready to . . .

Log On and Off Windows 7

1. Turn on your computer to begin the Windows 7 start-up sequence.

2. In the resulting Windows 7 Welcome screen, enter your password, if you've set one, and click the arrow button (or click Switch User and choose another user to log on as). Windows 7 verifies your password and displays the Windows 7 desktop, as shown in Figure 1-1. (*Note:* If you haven't set up the password protection feature or more than one user, you're taken directly to the Windows 7 desktop. For more on adding and changing passwords, see Chapter 14.)

3. To change to another user account, first save any open documents, close any open applications, and then choose Start. Then click the arrow next to the Shut Down button in the bottom-right corner of the Start menu and choose Log Off. Windows 7 logs off and displays a list of users. To log on again, click a user icon.

 To create another user, choose Start⇨Control Panel, and under the User Accounts and Family Safety heading, click Add or Remove User Accounts. Then click Create a New Account. Follow the instructions to enter a name for the account and set a password for it, if you like.

 See Chapter 14 for more detailed information about creating and managing user accounts.

Figure 1-1: The Windows 7 desktop

 After you set up more than one user, before you get to the password screen, you have to click the icon for the user you wish to log on as.

Work with the Start Menu

1. Press the ⊞ key on your keyboard or click the Start button on the desktop to display the Start menu (see Figure 1-2).

2. From the Start menu, you can do any of the following:

   - Click All Programs to display a list of all programs on your computer. You can click any program in the list to open it.

   - Click any category on the right of the Start menu to display a Windows Explorer window with related folders and files (see Figure 1-3).

   - Click either frequently used programs at the left of the Start menu, or click the arrow to the right of an application to display a list of recently used files and then click a file to open it in that application.

   - Click the Power button icon to close all programs and turn off Windows.

   - Click the arrow next to the Power button to display a menu of choices for putting your computer to sleep or using Hibernate mode (see the next Tip for more about these settings), restarting your computer, or for logging off or on as a different user.

3. When you move your cursor away from the Start menu, it disappears.

 Putting your computer in Sleep mode is like pausing your computer without closing open documents and programs. Sleep still uses a bit of power and allows you to quickly get back to work after only a few seconds. Hibernate mode is mainly for laptops because it saves your battery life. When you choose Hibernate, open documents or program settings are saved to your hard drive, and your computer switches off. Your computer takes longer to boot up from Hibernate and have the Windows desktop display, but it saves more power than Sleep.

Figure 1-2: The Start Menu

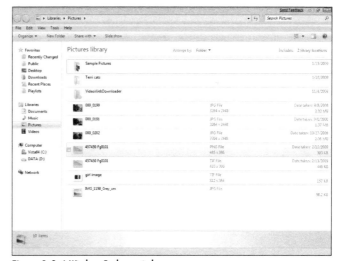

Figure 1-3: A Windows Explorer window

Work with Frequently Used Programs

1. If there are programs you use frequently, you can pin them to the taskbar area just to the right of the Start button (see Figure 1-4). When you first open Windows, this area may include icons for programs, such as the Internet Explorer and Windows Media Player, or a shortcut to open Windows Explorer.

2. To open any of these items, click its icon, and the window for that program opens. See Figure 1-5.

3. To close an item you've opened, click the Close button in the top-right corner of the window (with an X on it).

 To display additional items in the taskbar, right-click the application in the Start menu or on the desktop and then choose Pin to Taskbar. You can also drag a desktop icon to the taskbar. (If you want help creating a desktop shortcut, see the task, "Create a Desktop Shortcut," later in this chapter.)

Figure 1-4: The taskbar

Figure 1-5: Opening a program from the taskbar

 You can add other functions to the taskbar. Right-click a blank area of the taskbar and choose Properties. Click the Toolbars tab to display it. Select the check box for any of the additional items listed there, such as a browser Address bar, or Links.

Set the Date and Time

1. Press the ⊞ key on your keyboard to display the taskbar if it isn't visible. (By default the taskbar is not kept visible at all times, though you can change that setting.)

2. Right-click the Date/Time display on the far right of the taskbar and then choose Adjust Date/Time from the shortcut menu that appears.

3. In the Date and Time dialog box that appears (see Figure 1-6), click the Change Date and Time button. In the Date and Time Settings dialog box that appears, enter a new time in the Time field or use the up and down arrows next to that field to change the time. Click OK.

4. To change the time zone, click the Change Time Zone button, choose another option from the Time Zone drop-down list, and click OK.

5. Click OK to apply the new settings and close the dialog box.

Figure 1-6: The Date and Time dialog box

 If you don't want your computer to adjust for Daylight Saving Time, click Change Time Zone and click the Automatically Adjust Clock for Daylight Saving Time check box to turn off this feature.

 Another option for displaying the time or date is to add the Clock or Calendar gadgets to the Windows desktop. See Chapter 5 for more about using gadgets.

Arrange Icons on the Desktop

1. Right-click the desktop and choose View in the resulting shortcut menu; be sure that Auto Arrange Icons isn't selected, as shown in Figure 1-7. (If it is selected, deselect it before proceeding to the next step.)

2. Right-click the Windows 7 desktop. In the resulting shortcut menu, choose Sort By and then click the criteria for sorting your desktop shortcuts (see Figure 1-8).

Figure 1-7: The Desktop shortcut menu, View submenu

3. You can also click any icon and drag it to another location on the desktop — for example, to separate it from other desktop icons so you can find it easily.

 If you've rearranged your desktop by moving items hither, thither, and yon and you want your icons in orderly rows along the left side of your desktop, snap them into place with the Auto Arrange feature. Right-click the desktop and then choose View⇨ Auto Arrange Icons.

Figure 1-8: The Desktop shortcut menu, Sort By submenu

 To change the size of desktop icons, use the shortcut menu in Step 1 and choose Large Icons, Medium Icons, or Small Icons.

Create a Desktop Shortcut

1. Choose Start⇨All Programs and locate the program on the list of programs that appears.

2. Right-click an item, FreeCell for example, and choose Send To⇨Desktop (Create Shortcut) (see Figure 1-9).

3. The shortcut appears on the desktop (see Figure 1-10). Double-click the icon to open the application.

 Occasionally, Windows 7 offers to delete desktop icons that you haven't used in a long time. Let it. The desktop should be reserved for frequently used programs, files, and folders. You can always re-create shortcuts easily if you need them again.

 To clean up your desktop manually, right-click the desktop and choose Personalize. Click the Change Desktop Icons link to the left. In the Desktop Icon Setting dialog box that appears, click the Restore Default button, which returns to the original desktop shortcuts set up on your computer.

 You can create a shortcut for a brand new item by right-clicking the desktop, choosing New, and then choosing an item to place there, such as a text document, bitmap image, or contact. Then double-click the shortcut that appears and begin working on the file in the associated application.

Figure 1-9: The Send To shortcut menu

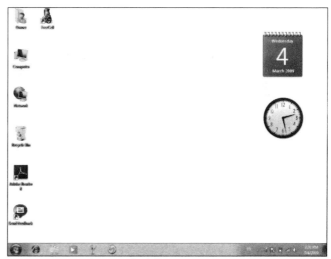

Figure 1-10: A new shortcut on the desktop

Empty the Recycle Bin

1. Right-click the Recycle Bin icon on the Windows 7 desktop and choose Empty Recycle Bin from the menu that appears (see Figure 1-11).

2. In the confirmation dialog box that appears (see Figure 1-12), click Yes. A progress dialog box appears indicating the contents are being deleted. Remember that after you empty the Recycle Bin, all the files in it are unavailable to you.

 Up until the moment you permanently delete items by performing the preceding steps, you can retrieve items in the Recycle Bin by right-clicking the desktop icon and choosing Open. Select the item you want to retrieve and then click the Restore This Item link near the top of the Recycle Bin window.

 You can modify the Recycle Bin properties by right-clicking it and choosing Properties. In the dialog box that appears, you can change the maximum size for the Recycle Bin and determine whether to immediately delete files you move to the Recycle Bin. You can also deselect the option of having a confirmation dialog box appear when you delete Recycle Bin contents.

Figure 1-11: The Recycle Bin shortcut menu

Figure 1-12: Confirming the Empty Recycle Bin command

Shut Down Your Computer

1. Choose Start and then click the arrow to the right of the Shut Down button.

2. In the resulting shortcut menu, shown in Figure 1-13, choose Hibernate to shut down the computer completely; if you want to *reboot* (turn off and turn back on) your computer, choose Restart.

Figure 1-13: The menu used to turn off or restart your computer

 If you're going away for a while but don't want to have to go through the whole booting up sequence complete with Windows 7 music when you return, you don't have to turn off your computer. Just click the Sleep command instead (in Step 2) to put your computer into a kind of sleeping state where the screen goes black and the fan shuts down. When you get back, just click your mouse button or press Enter, or in some cases (especially on some laptops), press the Power button; your computer springs to life, and whatever programs and documents you had open are still open.

 If your computer freezes up for some reason, you can turn it off in a couple of ways. Press Ctrl+Alt+Delete twice in a row, or press the power button on your CPU and hold it until the computer shuts down.

 Don't simply turn off your computer at the power source unless you have to because of a computer dysfunction. Windows might not start up properly the next time you turn it on if you don't follow the proper shutdown procedure.

Controlling Applications with Windows 7

You might think of Windows 7 as a set of useful accessories, such as games, a calculator, and a paint program for playing around with images, but Windows 7 is first and foremost an operating system. Windows 7's main purpose is to enable you to run and manage other software applications, from programs that manage your finances to the latest 3-D computer action game. By using the best methods for accessing and running software with Windows 7, you save time; setting up Windows 7 in the way that works best for you can make your life easier.

In this chapter, you explore several simple and very handy techniques for launching and moving between applications. You go through step-by-step procedures ranging from opening an application to resizing application windows to removing programs when you no longer need them.

This is where you explore all the procedures that you can use to launch, move among, and close applications with Windows 7.

Get ready to . . .

Launch an Application

1. Launch an application by using any of the following four methods:

   • Choose Start⇨All Programs. Locate the program name on the All Programs list that appears and click it. Clicking an item with a folder icon displays a list of programs within it; just click the program on that sublist to open it (as shown in Figure 2-1).

   • Double-click a program shortcut icon on the desktop (see Figure 2-2).

   • Click an item on the taskbar. The taskbar should display by default; if it doesn't, press the ⊞ key (on your keyboard) to display it and then click an icon on the taskbar (as shown in Figure 2-2), just to the right of the Start button. See Chapter 1 for more about working with the taskbar.

   • If you used the program recently and saved a document, choose it from the list of recently used programs displayed when you first open the Start menu. Then click a document created in that program from the list that displays. (See Chapter 1 for information about displaying recently used files on the Start menu.)

2. When the application opens, if it's a game, play it; if it's a spreadsheet, enter numbers into it; if it's your e-mail program, start deleting junk mail. . . . You get the idea.

 Not every program that's installed on your computer appears as a desktop shortcut or taskbar icon. To add a program to the taskbar or to add a desktop shortcut, see Chapter 1.

Figure 2-1: The All Programs menu

Figure 2-2: Desktop shortcuts and shortcuts on the taskbar

Resize Application Windows

1. When you open an application window, it can be maximized to fill the whole screen, restored down to a smaller window, or minimized to an icon on the taskbar. With an application open and maximized, click the Restore Down button (the icon showing two overlapping windows) in the top-right corner of the program window (see Figure 2-3). The window reduces in size.

2. To enlarge a window that's been restored down to again fill the screen, click the Maximize button. (*Note:* This button is the same location as the Restore Down button; this button changes its name to one or the other, depending on whether you have the screen reduced in size or maximized. A ScreenTip identifies the button when you pass your mouse over it.)

3. Click the Minimize button (it's to the left of the Restore Down/Maximize button and looks like a small bar) to minimize the window to an icon on the taskbar. To open the window again, click the taskbar icon.

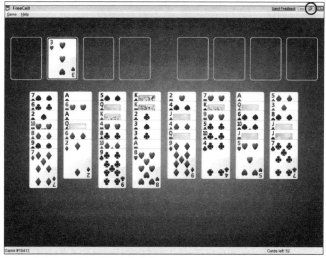

Figure 2-3: A maximized FreeCell window

 With a window maximized, you can't move the window. If you reduce a window in size, you can then click and hold the title bar to drag the window around the desktop, which is one way to view more than one window on your screen at the same time. You can also click and drag the corners of a reduced window to resize it to any size you want.

Switch between Running Applications

1. Open two or more programs. The last program that you open is the active program.

2. Press Alt+Tab to move from one open application window to another.

3. Press and hold Alt+Tab to open a small box, as shown in Figure 2-4, revealing all opened programs.

4. Release the Tab key but keep the Alt key pressed down. Press the Tab key to cycle through the icons representing open programs.

5. Release the Alt key, and Windows 7 switches to whichever program is selected. To switch back to the last program that was active, simply press Alt+Tab, and that program becomes the active program once again.

Figure 2-4: The list of active programs

All open programs also appear as items on the Windows 7 taskbar. Just click any running program on the taskbar to display that window and make it the active program. If the taskbar isn't visible, press the ⊞ key on your keyboard to display it.

Move Information between Applications

1. Open documents in two applications (see the next task for more about opening applications). If their windows are maximized, click the Restore Down buttons in the upper-right corners to reduce their sizes.

2. Click the bottom-right corner of each program window and drag to change the size further until you can see both programs on the Windows desktop at once (see Figure 2-5).

3. Click and hold their title bars to drag the windows around your desktop, or right-click the taskbar and choose Cascade Windows, Show Windows Stacked, or Show Windows Side by Side to automatically arrange the windows on the desktop.

4. Select the information that you want to move (for example, text, numbers, or a graphical object in a document) and drag it to the other application document (see Figure 2-6).

5. Release your mouse, and the information is copied to the document in the destination window.

 You can also use simple cut-and-paste or copy-and-paste operations to take information from one application and move it or place a copy of it into a document in another application. To do this, first click and drag over the information in a document and then press Ctrl+X to cut or Ctrl+C to copy the item. Click in the destination document where you want to place the item and press Ctrl+V.

 Remember, this won't work between every type of application. For example, you can't click and drag an open picture in Paint into the Windows Calendar. It will most dependably work when dragging text or objects from one Office or other standard word processing, presentation, database, or spreadsheet program to another.

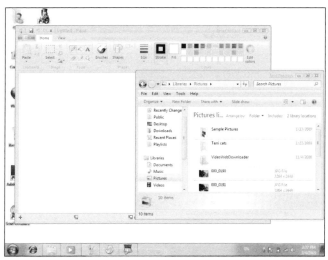

Figure 2-5: Arranging windows

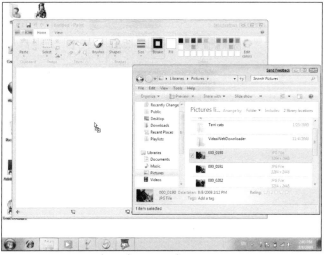

Figure 2-6: Dragging a selection between windows

Start an Application Automatically

1. Choose Start⇨All Programs.

2. Right-click the Startup folder and choose Open (see Figure 2-7).

3. Right-click Start and choose Open Windows Explorer. In the window that appears, locate and open the folder where the application you want to start when you start Windows is located. Click to select it.

4. Drag the item to the Startup window you opened in Step 2. The program appears in the Startup folder (see Figure 2-8).

5. When you finish moving programs into the Startup folder, click the Close button in the upper-right corner of both windows. The programs you moved will now open every time you start Windows 7. You can remove an application from Startup folder by right-clicking it and choosing Delete.

 If you place too many programs in Startup, it might take a minute or two before you can get to work because you have to wait for programs to load. Don't overfill your Startup folder: Use it just for the programs you need most often.

 You can also move documents that you work on frequently, for example a household budget or major project schedule, into the Startup folder so you can access them quickly.

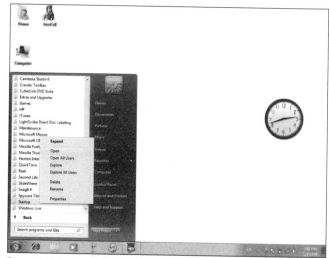

Figure 2-7: Opening the Startup folder

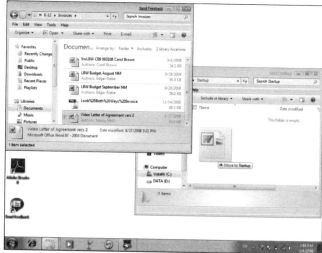

Figure 2-8: The Startup folder contents

Close an Application

1. With an application open, first save any open documents (typically you can choose File⇨Save to do this, though in recent Microsoft Office products, you click the application button and choose Save or Save As) and then close the application by using one of these methods:

   • Click the Close button in the upper-right corner of the window.

   • Press Alt+F4 to close an active open window.

   • Choose File (or application button)⇨Exit (see Figure 2-9).

2. The application closes. If you haven't saved changes in any open documents before trying to close the application, you see a dialog box asking whether you want to save the document(s) (see Figure 2-10). Click Save or Don't Save, depending on whether you want to save your changes.

 To save a new document for the first time, before closing an application choose File⇨Save and use settings in the Save dialog box (that appears) to name the file and also specify which folder to save it to.

 Note that choosing File⇨Exit closes all open documents in an application. Choose File⇨Close to close only the currently active document and keep the application and any other open documents open.

Figure 2-9: Choosing the Exit command

Figure 2-10: Saving changes to open documents

 You don't have to close an application to open or switch to another. To switch between open applications, press Alt+Tab and use the arrow keys to move to the application (or document if multiple documents are open in an application) in which you want to work.

Set Program Defaults

1. Choose Start⇨Control Panel⇨Programs.

2. In the resulting Programs window, as shown in Figure 2-11, click the Set Your Default Programs link in the Default Programs section to see specifics about the programs that are set as defaults.

3. In the resulting Set Default Programs window, click a program in the list on the left (see Figure 2-12) and then click the Set This Program as Default option. You can also click Choose Defaults for This Program and select specific file types (such as the `.jpeg` graphics file format or the `.docx` Word 2007 file format) to open in this program; click Save after you've made these selections.

4. Click OK to save your settings.

 You can also choose which devices to use by default to play media, such as movies or audio files, by selecting Change Default Settings for Media or Devices in the Programs window you opened in Step 1 above.

Figure 2-11: The Programs window

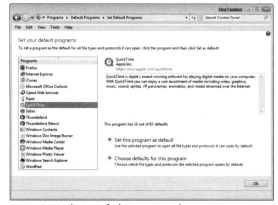

Figure 2-12: The Set Default Programs window

Remove an Application

1. Choose Start⇨Control Panel⇨Uninstall a Program (under the Programs category).

2. In the resulting Uninstall or Change a Program window, as shown in Figure 2-13, click a program and then click the Uninstall (or sometimes this is labeled Uninstall/ Change) button. Although some programs will display their own uninstall screen, in most cases, a confirmation dialog box appears (see Figure 2-14).

3. If you're sure that you want to remove the program, click Yes in the confirmation dialog box. A dialog box shows the progress of the procedure; it disappears when the program has been removed.

4. Click the Close button to close the Uninstall or Change a Program window.

 With some programs that include multiple applications, such as Microsoft Office, you get both an Uninstall and a Change option in Step 2. That's because you might want to remove only one program, not the whole shooting match. For example, you might decide that you have no earthly use for Access but can't let a day go by without using Excel and Word — so why not free up some hard drive space and send Access packing? If you want to modify a program in this way, click the Change button in Step 2 of this task rather than the Uninstall button. The dialog box that appears allows you to select the programs that you want to install or uninstall or might open the original installation screen from your software program.

 Warning: If you click the Change or Uninstall button, some programs will simply be removed with no further input from you. Be really sure that you don't need a program before you remove it, or that you have the original software on disc so you can reinstall it should you need it again.

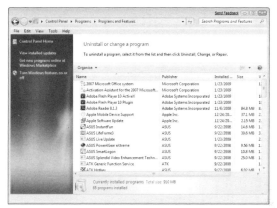

Figure 2-13: The Uninstall or Change a Program window

Figure 2-14: The removal confirmation dialog box

 If you used some earlier versions of Windows, note that the Add a Program command is gone. Because all software created today allows you to put a CD/DVD into your drive or download it from the Internet and then follow onscreen directions to install the program, Microsoft must have decided that its own Add a Program feature was obsolete!

Working with Files and Folders

*J*oin me for a moment in the office of yesteryear. Notice all the metal filing cabinets and manila file folders holding paper rather than the sleek computer workstations and wireless Internet connections we use today.

Fast forward: You still organize the work you do every day in files and folders, but today, the metal and cardboard have been dropped in favor of electronic bits and bytes. *Files* are the individual documents that you save from within applications, such as Word and Excel, and you use folders and subfolders to organize several files into groups or categories, such as by project or by customer.

In this chapter, you find out how to organize and work with files and folders, including

➡ **Finding your way around files and folders:** This includes tasks such as locating and opening files and folders.

➡ **Manipulating files and folders:** These tasks cover moving, renaming, deleting, and printing a file.

➡ **Squeezing a file's contents:** This involves creating a compressed folder to reduce a large file to a more manageable creature.

Access Recently Used Items from the Start Menu

1. Open the Start menu and right-click any blank area. From the resulting shortcut menu, choose Properties.

2. In the Taskbar and Start Menu Properties dialog box that appears, click the Start Menu tab (if that tab isn't already displayed).

3. Make sure that the Store and Display Recently Opened Items in the Start Menu and the Taskbar check box is selected (see Figure 3-1) and then click OK.

4. Open the Start menu and hover your mouse over any recently opened program listed on the left side that has an arrow, and then a submenu of recently opened items appears to the right. Choose a file from the Recent submenu (see Figure 3-2) to open it.

 Recently opened programs should be displayed in the Start menu by default, but if they aren't, follow directions in Step 1 to open the Taskbar and Start Menu Properties dialog box and make sure that the Store and Display Recently Opened Programs in the Start Menu check box is selected.

Figure 3-1: The Taskbar and Start Menu Properties dialog box

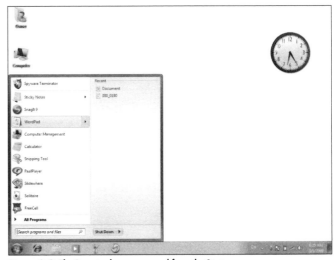

Figure 3-2: The Recent submenu accessed from the Start menu

Locate Files and Folders in Your Computer

1. Choose Start⇨Computer.

2. In the resulting Computer window (see Figure 3-3), double-click an item, such as a USB drive, a CD-ROM drive, or your computer hard drive, to open it.

3. If the file or folder that you want is stored within another folder (see Figure 3-4 for an example of the resulting window), double-click the folder or a series of folders until you locate it.

4. When you find the file you want, double-click it to open it.

 Note the buttons on the top of the window in Figure 3-4. Use the commands in this area to perform common file and folder tasks, such as organizing, sharing, or opening files.

 Depending on how you choose to display files and folders, you might see text listings as in Figure 3-4, icons, or even thumbnail representations of file contents. Use the View menu in the Computer window to configure how to display files and folders.

Figure 3-3: The Computer window

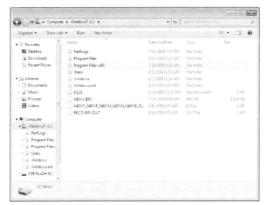

Figure 3-4: The window for a hard drive

Locate Files and Folders in Windows Explorer

1. Right-click the Start menu and choose Open Windows Explorer, or click the Windows Explorer button on the taskbar (it looks like a set of folders).

2. In the resulting Windows Explorer window, as shown in Figure 3-5, double-click a folder in the main window or in the list along the left side to open the folder.

3. The folder's contents are displayed. If necessary, open a series of folders in this manner until you locate the file you want.

4. When you find the file you want, double-click it to open it.

 To see different perspectives and information about files in Windows Explorer, click the arrow on the Views button (it looks like a series of columns) and choose one of the following menu options: Extra Large, Large Icons, Medium Icons, or Small Icons for graphical displays; List; Details to show details, such as Date Modified and Size; Tiles to show the file/folder name, type, and size; and Content to display only the date modified and file size. If you're working with a folder containing graphics files, the graphics automatically display as thumbnails unless you choose Details.

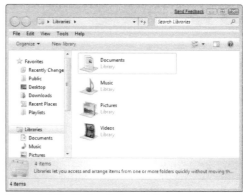

Figure 3-5: The Windows Explorer window

 There are some shortcuts to commonly used folders in the Start menu, including Documents, Pictures, Music, and Games. Click one of these, and Windows Explorer opens that particular window.

Search for a File

1. Open the Start menu and type a search term in the search field at the bottom.

2. A list of search results appears divided by the location of the results (see Figure 3-6).

3. Click the See More Results link.

4. In the Search Results in Indexed Locations window that appears (see Figure 3-7), click View to cycle through the options of various size icons or text listings.

5. When you locate the file you want, double-click it to open it.

 Search Folders were a new feature in Windows Vista that has carried over to Windows 7. To save the results of a search, you can click the Save Search button. In the Save As dialog box that appears, provide a filename and type, set the location to save it to, and then click Save. The search results are saved as a search folder on your computer in your username folder.

 Choose the Folder and Search Options command from the Organize menu in the Search Results in Indexed Locations window, as shown in Figure 3-7, to modify Search settings. In the Search tab in the Folder Options dialog box that appears, indicate what locations to search, whether to find partial matches for search terms, and more.

Figure 3-6: The Search field and results in the Start menu

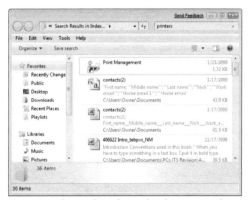

Figure 3-7: The Search Results in Indexed Locations window

Move a File or Folder

1. Right-click the Start menu button and choose Open Windows Explorer.

2. In the resulting Windows Explorer window (see Figure 3-8), double-click a folder or series of folders to locate the file that you want to move.

3. Take one of the following actions:

    *   Click and drag the file to another folder in the Folders pane on the left side of the window. If you right-click and drag, you're offered the options of moving, copying, or creating a shortcut to the item when you place it via a shortcut menu that appears.

    *   Right-click the file and choose Send To. Then choose from the options shown in the submenu that appears (as shown in Figure 3-9).

4. Click the Close button in the upper-right corner of the Windows Explorer window to close it.

 If you change your mind about moving an item using the right-click-and-drag method, you can click Cancel on the shortcut menu that appears.

 If you want to create a copy of a file or folder in another location on your computer, right-click the item and choose Copy. Use Windows Explorer to navigate to the location where you want to place a copy, right-click, and choose Paste or press Ctrl+V.

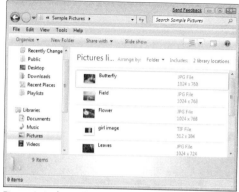

Figure 3-8: The Windows Explorer window

Figure 3-9: The Send To submenu

Rename a File or Folder

1. Locate the file that you want to rename by using Windows Explorer. (Right-click Start and choose Open Windows Explorer.)

2. Right-click the file and choose Rename (see Figure 3-10).

3. The filename is now available for editing. Type a new name and then click anywhere outside the filename to save the new name.

 You can't rename a file to have the same name as another file located in the same folder. To give a file the same name as another, cut it from its current location, paste it into another folder, and then follow the procedure in this task. Or, open the file and save it to a new location with the same name, which creates a copy. Be careful, though: Two files with the same name can cause confusion when you search for files. If at all possible, use unique filenames.

Create a Shortcut to a File or Folder

1. Locate the file or folder by using Windows Explorer. (Right-click Start and choose Open Windows Explorer.)

2. In the resulting Windows Explorer window (see Figure 3-11), right-click the file or folder that you want to create a shortcut for and then choose Send To⇨Desktop (Create Shortcut).

3. A shortcut named Shortcut to *File or Folder Name* appears above the original item. Click the shortcut and drag it to the desktop.

 After you place a shortcut on the desktop, to open the file in its originating application or a folder in Windows Explorer, simply double-click the desktop shortcut icon.

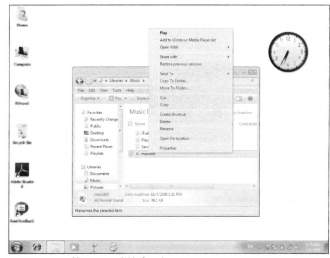

Figure 3-10: A filename available for editing

Figure 3-11: The Windows Explorer window displaying a shortcut menu

Print a File

1. Open the file in the application that it was created in.

2. Choose File⇨Print (note that with more recent versions of Office programs, you click the Office button and then choose Print).

3. In the resulting Print dialog box (see Figure 3-12), select what to print; these options might vary but generally include the following

   - **All** prints all pages in the document.

   - **Current Page** prints whatever page your cursor is active in at the moment.

   - **Pages** prints a page range or series of pages you enter in that field. For example, enter **3-11** to print pages 3 through 11; or enter **3, 7, 9-11** to print pages 3, 7, and 9 through 11.

   - **Selection** prints any text or objects that you've selected within the file when you choose the Print command.

4. In the Number of Copies field, click the up or down arrow to set the number of copies to make; if you want multiple copies collated, select the Collate check box.

5. Click OK to proceed with printing.

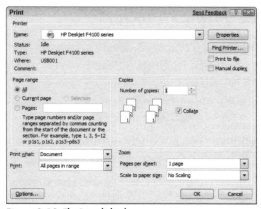

Figure 3-12: The Print dialog box

 Here's another method for printing: Locate the file by using Windows Explorer (right-click Start and choose Open Windows Explorer). Right-click the file and choose Print from the shortcut menu that appears. The file prints with your default printer settings.

 Different applications might offer different options in the Print dialog box. For example, PowerPoint offers several options for what to print, including slides, handouts, or the presentation outline, and Outlook allows you to print e-mails in table or in memo style.

Delete a File or Folder

1. Locate the file or folder by using Windows Explorer. (Right-click Start and choose Open Windows Explorer.)

2. In the resulting Windows Explorer window, right-click the file or folder that you want to delete (see Figure 3-13) and then choose Delete.

3. In the resulting dialog box (see Figure 3-14), click Yes to delete the file.

 When you delete a file or folder in Windows, it's not really gone. It's removed to the Recycle Bin. Windows periodically purges older files from this folder, but you might still be able to retrieve recently deleted files and folders from it. To try to restore a deleted file or folder, double-click the Recycle Bin icon on the desktop. Right-click the file or folder and choose Restore. Windows restores the file to wherever it was when you deleted it.

 Instead of right-clicking and choosing Delete from the menu that appears in Step 2 above, you can click the Delete key on your keyboard.

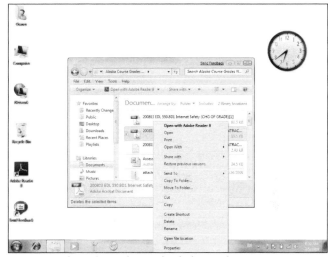

Figure 3-13: The Windows Explorer window displaying a shortcut menu

Figure 3-14: The Delete File confirmation dialog box

Create a Compressed File or Folder

1. Locate the files or folders that you want to compress by using Windows Explorer. (Right-click Start and choose Open Windows Explorer.)

2. In the resulting Windows Explorer window, you can do the following (as shown in Figure 3-15):

   • **Select a series of files or folders:** Click a file or folder, press and hold Shift to select a series of items listed consecutively in the folder, and click the final item.

   • **Select nonconsecutive items:** Press the Ctrl key and click the items.

3. Right-click the selected items. In the resulting shortcut menu (see Figure 3-16), choose Send To⇨Compressed (Zipped) Folder. A new compressed folder appears below the last selected file in the Windows Explorer list. The folder icon is named after the last file you selected in the series.

 You might want to rename a compressed folder with a name other than the one that Windows automatically assigns to it. See the task "Rename a File or Folder," earlier in this chapter, to find out just how to do that.

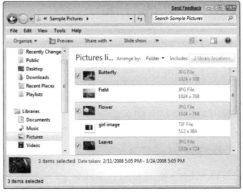

Figure 3-15: A series of selected files and folders

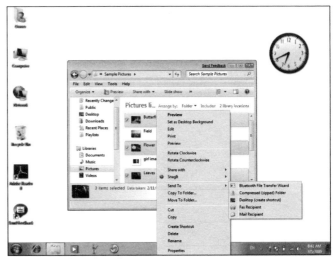

Figure 3-16: The Send To submenu

Add a File to Your Favorites List

1. Locate the files or folders that you want to make Favorites by using Windows Explorer. (Right-click Start and choose Open Windows Explorer.)

2. In the resulting Windows Explorer window, click a file or folder and drag it to any of the Favorites folders in the Folders pane on the left (see Figure 3-17).

3. To see a list of your Favorites, choose Start⇨Favorites.

4. In the resulting submenu (see Figure 3-18), click an item to open it.

 If the Favorites item doesn't display on your Start menu, right-click the Start menu and choose Properties. On the Start Menu tab with Start Menu selected, click the Customize button. Make sure that Favorites Menu is selected and then click OK twice to save the setting.

Figure 3-17: The Favorites folders in Windows Explorer

Figure 3-18: The Favorites submenu on the Windows Start menu

Using Built-In Windows Applications

Windows 7 isn't just a traffic cop for your computer's hardware and other software programs; it has its own set of neat tools that you can use to get things done. What sorts of things? Well, by using various *Windows Accessories* (that is, built-in software programs), you can do everything from writing down great thoughts to working with beautiful pictures. Here's what the Windows built-in applications help you do:

➡ **Work with words.** WordPad provides a virtual pad for jotting down ideas, making notes, creating small documents, or entering programming code. WordPad isn't as robust as some mainstream word processors, but it's just write (pun intended) for simple documents with a few formatting bells and whistles.

➡ **Play with images.** Windows makes you an artist because you can view and edit graphics files in Paint and view digital images (you know, the photos you took at little Ricky's birthday party?) in the Windows Photo Viewer. The new Snipping Tool is a way to grab little clippings of either words or images, annotate them, and then add them to a variety of documents.

➡ **Manage numbers and make notes.** Windows Calculator is an electronic version of that little plastic calculator you carry around; it's a great place to work with figures on the fly. Windows Sticky Notes are like virtual Post-It Notes. You can type a note and stick it on your desktop so you won't forget that appointment or to-do item.

Create a Formatted Document in WordPad

1. Choose Start➪All Programs➪Accessories➪WordPad to open the WordPad window, as shown in Figure 4-1.

2. Enter text in the blank document. (*Note:* Press Enter to create blank lines between paragraphs.)

3. Click and drag to select the text; then click the Home tab to display font settings (if it's not already displayed).

4. With the font settings shown in Figure 4-2, adjust the settings for Font, Font Style, or Size. You can apply subscript or superscript effects by selecting those buttons. You can also modify the font color and change the font background color.

5. Click various other tools, such as the alignment buttons or the Bullets button on the Ribbon, to format selected text.

6. Click the Picture button in the Insert area of the Home tab on the Ribbon to insert a picture.

7. In the Select Picture dialog box that appears, click an image in your Picture folder (or search for an image stored elsewhere on your computer using the folder pane on the left) and then click Open. Modify the inserted object however you want (moving it or resizing it, for example).

8. When your document is complete, click the Save button in the top-left part of the window (it looks like a little disk). In the Save As dialog box, enter a name in the File Name text box, select a file location from the Address Bar drop-down list, and then click Save.

Figure 4-1: The Windows WordPad window

Figure 4-2: The WordPad Font tools

 E-mailing a copy of your WordPad document is simplicity itself. Just click the WordPad button (located near the top-left corner and shaped like a little document with lines on it) and click Send E-mail. An e-mail form appears from your default e-mail program with the file already attached. Just enter a recipient and a message and click Send. It's on its way!

Edit a Picture in Paint

1. Choose Start➪All Programs➪Accessories➪Paint.

2. In the resulting Paint window, click the Paint button (near the top-left corner with a picture of a little document on it) and choose Open. Locate a picture file that you want to edit (see Figure 4-3), select it, and click Open. You see a pretty picture of my cats in the Paint window in Figure 4-4.

3. Now you can edit the picture in any number of ways:

   - **Edit colors.** Choose a color from the color palette on the Home tab of the Paint window and use various tools (such as Brushes, Fill with Color, and the Pick Color dropper) to apply color to the image or selected drawn objects, such as rectangles.

   - **Select areas.** Click the Select button and then choose a selection shape, either Rectangular or Free-Form. Click and drag on the image to select portions of the picture. You can then crop to only the selected elements by clicking the crop tool.

   - **Add text.** Click the Text button, and then click and drag the image to create a text box in which you can enter and format text.

   - **Draw objects.** Click the Shapes button and choose shapes, such as Rectangle, Rounded Rectangle, Polygon, or Ellipse, and then click and drag on the image to draw that shape.

   - **Modify the image.** Use the buttons on the Image section of the Ribbon to stretch out, flip around, or change the size of the image.

4. Click the Save button to save your masterpiece, or click the Paint button and choose Print to print it, or File➪ Send in an e-mail to send it by e-mail.

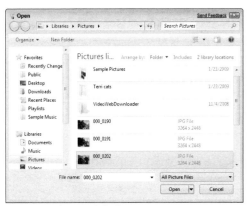

Figure 4-3: The Open dialog box

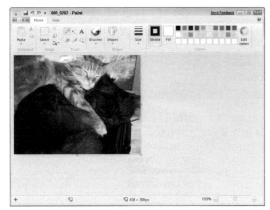

Figure 4-4: A picture opened in Paint

Not happy with the colors that Paint shows you on its color palette? Do you want to use a particular shade of fire engine red for the hair on your drawing of a pop star? To change the colors available to you on the color palette, click the Edit Colors button. Click various colors to add to the palette and then click the Add to Custom Colors button and click OK to save the modified palette.

View a Digital Image in the Windows Photo Viewer

1. Right-click the Start button and choose Open Windows Explorer.

2. In the resulting window, double-click the Pictures Library icon. Double-click any photo in the Pictures Library folder. In the Windows Photo Viewer window, as shown in Figure 4-5, you can use the tools at the bottom (see Figure 4-6) to do any of the following:

   • The Next and Previous icons move to a previous or following image in the same folder.

   • The Display Size icon in the shape of a magnifying glass displays a slider you can click and drag to change the size of the image thumbnails.

   • The Delete button deletes the selected image.

   • The Rotate Clockwise and Rotate Counterclockwise icons spin the image 90 degrees at a time.

   • The center Play Slide Show button with a slide image on it displays the images in your Picture folder in a continuous slide show.

Figure 4-5: The Windows Photo Viewer

Figure 4-6: The tools you can use to manipulate images

 Did you upload a photo from your camera but you don't remember what you called it? If you want to find a photo you imported to the Pictures Library from a camera or scanner in the recent past, click the Recently Imported folder in the picture list on the left.

3. Use any of the buttons at the top of the window (see Figure 4-7) to do the following:

   • **File** displays commands for working with the file, such as Delete and Rename.

   • **Print** is the button to click to print the selected image.

   • **E-mail** opens a dialog box to specify the image to be attached to an e-mail using your default mail program.

   • **Burn** allows you to create a DVD, movie, or data disc using the image.

   • **Open** allows you to open the image in another program, such as Paint, which you can use to edit the image.

4. When you finish viewing and working with images, click the Close button in the top right-hand corner to close the Photo Viewer (see Figure 4-8).

Figure 4-7: Use these buttons and drop-down lists to work with your photos in a variety of ways

Figure 4-8: Close the Windows Photo Viewer

 If you want prints of your photos, here's a handy shortcut. Choose Order Prints from the Print button drop-down list. You can download a list of online printing companies, such as Fujifilm, Shutterfly, or CVS Pharmacy and order prints online.

Clip with the Windows Snipping Tool

1. Choose Start➪All Programs➪Accessories➪Snipping Tool.

2. In the Snipping Tool window that appears (see Figure 4-9), click the down-arrow on the New button and choose a snip mode from the drop-down list:

   - **Free Form Snip** lets you draw any old kind of line you like, such as a triangle, to define what you want to snip.

   - **Rectangular Snip** does what it says: When you click and drag over a region, it forms a rectangular snip.

   - **Windows Snip** allows you to select an active window to snip.

   - **Full-Screen Snip** takes the entire enchilada, capturing the whole screen in the wink of an eye.

3. If you chose Free Form or Rectangular in Step 2, click and drag on the desktop or in a document to form an area to snip. If you chose Windows, click the window you want to snip. If you chose Full-Screen, the snip happens automatically.

4. In the mark-up window that appears (see Figure 4-10), use the Pen, Highlighter, and Eraser tools to mark up or modify the image.

5. Click the Save Snip button that looks like a computer disk to display the Save As dialog box, where you can enter a filename, specify the location to save the file to, and then click Save.

Figure 4-9: The Snipping Tool window

Figure 4-10: The mark-up window with a captured snip

Add Sticky Notes

1. Choose Start⇨All Programs⇨Accessories⇨Sticky Notes.

2. In the Sticky Note that appears (see Figure 4-11), type a note or cut/copy and paste text into the note from another document. To add another note, click the New Note button (it has a plus sign on it).

3. With a Sticky Note on your desktop, you can click the title bar across the top of a note and drag it wherever you wish.

4. To delete a Sticky Note, click the Delete Note button (which sports an X) and choose Yes from the Delete Note dialog box that appears.

 Right-click a Sticky Note to choose a different color. You can create your own color scheme in this way so that purple notes might be appointments, green notes might be reminders about bills, pink notes might remind you of social obligations, and so on.

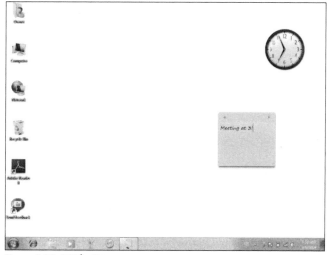

Figure 4-11: A Sticky Note

Track Numbers with Windows Calculator

Figure 4-12: The Calculator window

1. Choose Start⇨All Programs⇨Accessories⇨Calculator.

2. In the Calculator window, as shown in Figure 4-12, click numbers and use the calculation symbols to perform a calculation. For example, click the 5, 8, and 9 buttons to enter 589; click the + button and then click the 9 button; click the = button to get the result of adding 589 to 9. (*Note:* Use the / symbol to divide, and the asterisk symbol to multiply.)

3. If you enter the wrong number, click the CE button to clear that entry. If you want to clear a calculation and begin a new one, click the C button.

4. Click the Mode menu to choose different types of calculators, such as scientific or statistics.

5. Click the Close button to close the Calculator.

 If you want to view a history of your calculations, much like an adding machine tape, choose Edit⇨History.

 You can get help with some standard calculations by choosing Options⇨Templates. This displays a worksheet pane with gas mileage, lease estimation, and mortgage estimation tools.

Using the Windows Gadget Gallery and Gadgets

*W*indows 7 has a *Windows Gadget Gallery* desktop feature. The Gallery contains tools, or *gadgets*, displayed as icons on the desktop. With gadgets, you can quickly access various handy features to check the weather, organize your calendar, feed online data directly to your desktop, and more. Here are some of the things you can do with the Windows gadgets that I cover in this chapter:

➡ **Work with images.** The Slide Show gadget is a continuous slide show of the photos in your Pictures folder.

➡ **Organize your time.** The Calendar gadget displayed on your desktop helps you keep track of the days, weeks, and months. The Clock gadget displays the time with an old-style wall clock and allows you to make changes to your time zone.

➡ **Play with puzzles.** A neat little Picture Puzzle gadget allows you to play a game that's so tiny, even your boss won't notice you're not actually working.

➡ **Work with online data.** The Feed Headlines gadget allows you to grab data from online RSS feeds (a format used for syndication of news and other content), such as the latest news or other useful information. Stocks and Currency Conversion gadgets provide up-to-the-minute data on stocks and currency values.

➡ **Keep an eye on your system performance.** The CPU Meter gadget provides up-to-date information about your computer processor speed and available memory.

Get ready to . . .

Open the Gadget Gallery and Add Gadgets to the Desktop

1. Right-click the desktop and choose Gadgets to open the Gadget Gallery window, as shown in Figure 5-1. Note that the gadgets that are included in your gallery may vary depending on your computer manufacturer.

2. Click any gadget and drag it to the desktop (see Figure 5-2).

3. Click the Close button to close the Gadget Gallery.

 Gadgets are hot, and people are creating more all the time. Click the Get More Gadgets Online link in the Gadget Gallery to scope out the latest gadgets and then download them.

 If you want to send a gadget away, just place your mouse over it and then click the Close button (marked with an X) that appears next to it. The gadget closes. Just follow the steps above to display it on the desktop again at any time.

Figure 5-1: The Gadget Gallery

Figure 5-2: Gadgets displayed on the desktop

Check the Time

1. Right-click the desktop and choose Gadgets.

2. In the Gadget Gallery that appears, click the clock and drag it to the desktop.

3. To make changes to the clock style or change the time zone, place your mouse over the clock and click the Settings button (it sports a little wrench symbol).

4. In the resulting Clock window (see Figure 5-3), click the Next or Previous buttons to move through the various available clock styles.

5. If you wish, you can enter a name for the clock in the Clock Name field. To change the time zone, click the arrow in the Time Zone field and choose your local time.

6. Click OK to save the clock settings.

 You can display a second hand on your clock by clicking the Show the Second Hand check box in the Clock settings dialog box.

Figure 5-3: The Clock gadget settings dialog box

 If you're on the road and want to keep track of the local time and the time back home, you can display more than one clock by simply dragging the Clock gadget to the desktop from the Gadget Gallery again. Make changes to the time zone settings and even use two different clock styles to tell them apart at a glance.

Display a Continuous Slide Show

1. Add the Slide Show gadget to the desktop (see the earlier task, "Open the Gadget Gallery and Add Gadgets to the Desktop").

2. Move your mouse over the Slide Show gadget and use the tools along the bottom of the slide show (see Figure 5-4) to do the following:

   - Click the **View button** to display the current slide in the Windows Photo Viewer.

   - Click **Pause** to stop the slide show at the current slide.

   - Click **Previous** to go to the previous slide.

   - Click **Next** to go to the next slide.

3. Click the Settings button, which looks like a little wrench. In the resulting Slide Show dialog box (see Figure 5-5), select the picture folders to include in the slide show, or modify the number of seconds to display each slide or a transition effect to use between slides.

4. Click OK to close the dialog box.

 When you click the View button to display the current slide in Windows Photo Viewer, you can use tools to modify the image, print it, e-mail it, or even create a movie. See Chapter 4 for more about using Windows Photo Viewer.

Figure 5-4: The Slide Show toolbar

Figure 5-5: The Slide Show dialog box

Use the Windows Calendar

1. Add the Calendar gadget (see Figure 5-6) to the desktop. (See the earlier task, "Open the Gadget Gallery and Add Gadgets to the Desktop.")

2. Move your mouse over the calendar and click the Size tool shown in Figure 5-7 to move between the large size, which displays both the monthly and daily sections (as shown in Figure 5-7), and the smaller size, which displays only the daily display by default.

3. With the larger calendar displayed, click the Next or Previous arrows to move to another month; double-click a date to display it in the lower part of the calendar; and click the red tab in the lower-left corner to return to today's date in the lower area.

 If you prefer to use the smaller size calendar but want it to display the monthly rather than daily calendar, just double-click the small display, and it toggles between month and day.

 With the monthly display shown in the smaller size, you can jump to the daily display for a specific date by double-clicking that date in the monthly view.

Figure 5-6: The Calendar gadget

Figure 5-7: The Calendar gadget larger view

Play with Puzzles

1. Add the Picture Puzzle gadget to the desktop. (See the earlier task, "Open the Gadget Gallery and Add Gadgets to the Desktop.")

2. Click one of the tools along the top of the puzzle (see Figure 5-8) to do the following:

   - **Pause Timer** stops the automatic count of seconds of play.

   - **Show Picture** displays the completed picture; release it and you go back to where you were in the game.

   - **Solve** ends the game and displays the completed picture.

3. To play the game, click any piece adjacent to a blank square. The piece moves into the blank space. Keep clicking and moving pieces until you get the picture pieces arranged to form a picture.

4. Click the Settings button to the right of the puzzle to display its settings in the Picture Puzzle dialog box (see Figure 5-9).

5. Click the Previous or Next button to scroll through available pictures for the puzzle.

6. When you find the picture you want, click OK to close the dialog box.

Figure 5-8: The Picture Puzzle gadget

Figure 5-9: The Picture Puzzle dialog box

Convert Currency

1. Add the Currency Conversion gadget to the desktop. (See the earlier task, "Open the Gadget Gallery and Add Gadgets to the Desktop.")

2. Connect to the Internet to access the latest currency rates (as shown in Figure 5-10) and do any of the following.

   • Enter the number of dollars; the number of equivalent euros is displayed.

   • Click one of the currency names, and a list of available currencies appears (see Figure 5-11). Click another currency to change which currencies to convert from and to.

 To view the online source for the latest currency conversion rates, click the Data Providers link. The MoneyCentral page on MSN opens. Click the Banking tab and then click the Currency Exchange Rates link to view current rates.

 If you want, you can display several Currency Conversion gadgets to compare multiple currencies at the same time.

Figure 5-10: The Currency Conversion gadget connected to the Internet

Figure 5-11: Pick which currency you're converting

Use the Feed Headlines Gadget

1. Add the Feed Headlines gadget to the desktop. (See the earlier task, "Open the Gadget Gallery and Add Gadgets to the Desktop.")

2. Click the Feed Viewer gadget to connect to the default RSS feed (see Figure 5-12).

3. At the Web site that appears, you can view blog entries, submit an entry, or subscribe to additional feeds.

4. Click the Settings button. In the resulting Feed Headlines dialog box (see Figure 5-13), select the default feed.

5. Click OK to close the dialog box.

 Use the Show Next Set of Feeds and Show Previous Set of Feeds arrows that appear at the bottom of the Feed Headlines gadget when you move your mouse over it to scroll through available feeds.

Figure 5-12: The Feed Headlines gadget

Figure 5-13: The Feed Headlines dialog box

Get the Latest Stock Quotes

1. Add the Stocks gadget to the desktop. (See the earlier task, "Open the Gadget Gallery and Add Gadgets to the Desktop.")

2. Connect to the Internet; stock prices and stock exchange data are displayed (see Figure 5-14).

3. Move your mouse over the bottom of the gadget and click the Plus button that appears. In the resulting Stocks dialog box (see Figure 5-15), do any of the following:

   • Type a stock symbol in the Add Stock Symbol field and click Add to add a tracked stock.

   • Click an item in My Tracked Stocks and click the Delete button to delete it, or use the Move Up or Move Down arrow to change its position in the list.

4. Click OK to close the dialog box.

Figure 5-14: The Stock gadget on the desktop displaying stocks

Figure 5-15: The Stocks setting dialog box

 When you click and drag the Stocks gadget to your desktop, it expands and displays a graph at the bottom giving you hour-by-hour changes in the selected stock on active trading days, during trading hours.

Monitor Your CPU

1. Add the CPU Meter gadget (see Figure 5-16) to the desktop. (See the earlier task, "Open the Gadget Gallery and Add Gadgets to the Desktop.")

2. Use the readouts to monitor the following:

   - CPU (on the left) monitors how hard your CPU is working to process various programs and processes running on your computer.

   - Memory (on the right) monitors the percent of your computer memory that's being used.

 That's about all there is to CPU Meter! You can click the Size button to toggle between a larger and smaller version, but you can't make any settings for it. It's just a little reminder that helps you keep track of your computer's performance. If memory is almost at 100 percent, consider freeing some space. If the CPU is at a higher percentage, odds are you have lots of programs running, which could be slowing down your computer's performance; consider shutting down some!

Figure 5-16: The CPU Meter gadget

 If you want more detail about your computer memory usage, use the Start menu to display the Control Panel and choose System and Security. The System links allow you to monitor the processor speed and the amount of RAM (random access memory) available.

Part II
Getting on the Internet

The 5th Wave — By Rich Tennant

"Look at this, Mother! I customized the browser so I can navigate the Web the way I want to."

Accessing the Internet

*T*he Internet has become as integral to computing as a cellphone is to how a teenager communicates. The Internet is how people stay in touch, transfer files, share images and music, shop for goods and services, and research everything from aardvarks to zebras.

You can easily get connected to the Internet. Most Internet service providers (ISPs) provide software to set up your connection automatically. But you can connect in a few different ways, and you'll encounter a few different technologies. You might also need to tinker around with some settings to get things working just the way you want them to.

In this chapter, you find out how to make and manage Internet connections, including

➡ **Setting up your connection:** The New Connection Wizard helps you with this process. Then you can designate your default connection so that you log on to the Internet how you prefer.

➡ **Modifying settings:** Whether you use a TCP/IP or an always-on connection (such as cable or DSL), you discover the ins and outs of configuring them here as well as how to share your Internet connection with someone else.

➡ **Disconnecting:** When you've finished using the Internet, you may wish to disconnect, and here's where I tell you how.

Set Up a New ISP Internet Connection

1. Choose Start⇨Control Panel⇨Network and Internet.

2. In the resulting window, click Network and Sharing Center.

3. In the resulting Network and Sharing Center window (see Figure 6-1), click the Set Up a New Connection or Network link.

4. In the Choose a Connection dialog box, accept the default Connect to the Internet option by clicking Next.

5. If you already have a connection set up, a dialog box appears stating that you are already connected. Click Set Up a New Connection Anyway to proceed. In the resulting dialog box, click Next to accept the default option of No, Create a New Connection.

6. In the resulting dialog box, click to select a type of connection. (These steps follow the Broadband selection.)

7. In the resulting dialog box, as shown in Figure 6-2, enter your User Name, Password, and Connection Name (if you want to assign one) and then click Connect. Windows automatically detects the connection, and the Network and Sharing Center appears with your connection listed.

 In many cases, if you have a disc from your ISP, you don't need to follow the preceding steps. Just pop that DVD into your DVD-ROM drive, and in no time, a window appears that gives you the Network and Sharing Center window.

Figure 6-1: The Network and Sharing Center window

Figure 6-2: The Connect to the Internet Wizard window

Share an Internet Connection on a Network

1. You can use a piece of hardware — a router — to share a connection (follow the router manufacturer's manual to do this) or use the Windows Internet Connection Sharing feature covered in this task. Choose Start⇨ Control Panel⇨Network and Internet.

2. In the resulting window, click the Network and Sharing Center link.

3. In the resulting Network and Sharing Center window (refer to Figure 6-1), click the Manage Wireless Networks link.

4. In the resulting window (see Figure 6-3), click a connection and then click the Adapter Properties link.

5. In the Connection Properties dialog box, click the Sharing tab (see Figure 6-4).

6. Select the Allow Other Network Users to Connect through This Computer's Internet Connection check box.

7. If you want other people on your network to control the shared Internet connection by enabling or disabling it, select the Allow Other Network Users to Control or Disable the Shared Internet Connection check box.

8. Click OK and then close the Manage Wireless Networks window to save the shared connection settings.

 Users on your network also have to make some settings to use your shared connection. They have to configure settings for an Internet communications standard — TCP/IP (Transmission Control Protocol/Internet Protocol) — on their local area connections so that they get an IP connection automatically.

Figure 6-3: The Manage Wireless Networks window

Figure 6-4: Selected options in the Connection Properties dialog box

Configure a Wireless Connection

1. Whether you have a network set up in your home or business to connect to, or you want to connect to free wireless networks as you roam around, you can make settings for that connection. Choose Start⇨Control Panel⇨Network and Internet.

2. In the resulting window, click the Network and Sharing Center link.

3. In the resulting Network and Sharing Center window (refer to Figure 6-1), click the Manage Wireless Networks link.

4. In the resulting window (see Figure 6-5), right-click a connection and then choose Properties.

5. In the Wireless Network Properties dialog box, click the Connection tab (see Figure 6-6).

6. On the Connection tab, make any of the following selections:

   • **Connect Automatically When This Network Is in Range:** This option has Windows make a connection whenever it detects this network.

Figure 6-5: The Manage Wireless Networks window

- **Connect to a More Preferred Network if Available:** This option allows Windows to switch among preferred networks when Windows detects that one's within range. A preferred connection is any network you have connected to previously. Sometimes this causes Windows to switch back and forth among preferred networks, so you may want to turn off this setting to avoid that.

- **Connect Even if the Network Is Not Broadcasting Its Name (SSID):** The *SSID (Service Set Identifier)* is the public name of a network, although network SSIDs aren't always unique. For security reasons, you might not want to connect to a network that doesn't provide this identifier.

7. Click OK to close the Wireless Network Properties dialog box and then the Close button (the red button with an X on the top-right corner of the Manage Wireless Networks window) to close it.

Figure 6-6: The Manage Wireless Networks dialog box, Connection tab

 Although you can enter addresses manually in the Internet Protocol Properties dialog box, I recommend letting them be assigned automatically. That way, if your setup changes, you don't have to go back and manually modify addresses. This also saves you the hassle of having to manually configure certain settings. Don't want to worry about such techie things? Me, neither. That's why I just let addresses be assigned automatically.

Repair a Connection

1. Choose Start⇨Control Panel⇨Network and Internet.

2. In the resulting window, click the Network and Sharing Center link.

3. In the resulting window, click the Fix a Network Problem link.

4. In the Network and Internet window (see Figure 6-7), click the Internet Connections link and in the following Troubleshooting window, click Next to proceed.

5. A series of questions follows, as in the first window of the Network Troubleshooter Wizard, as shown in Figure 6-8. Respond to the questions to pin down your connection problem. If Windows suggests an action you must perform, such as plugging in a cable, do so.

 Sometimes diagnosing a connection doesn't do the trick. In that case, it's best to delete the connection and just create it again by clicking the Set Up a New Connection or Network link in the Network and Sharing Center window and entering the correct settings.

 You may have recently made or changed a setting that caused your network connection to fail. If that could be the case, you might consider running a System Restore to an earlier point in time. A *System Restore* takes you back to a time before you changed your settings, but it doesn't delete any programs or documents. See Chapter 18 for more about using the System Restore feature.

Figure 6-7: The Network and Internet window

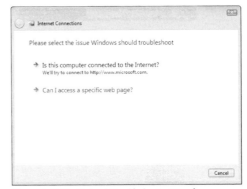

Figure 6-8: The Network Troubleshooter Wizard

Designate Home, Work, and Public Connections

1. Many people have both a home and work network that they connect to, and Windows can apply appropriate settings based on the type of connection you designate. In addition, when connecting to public networks, you might want to specify those connections as such for security reasons. Choose Start➪Control Panel➪Network and Internet.

2. In the resulting window, click the Network and Sharing Center link.

3. In the Network and Sharing Center window (see Figure 6-9), for any active connection, click the network type link listed under the network name (such as Work Network).

4. In the Set Network Location window (see Figure 6-10), click the appropriate setting:

   • **Home Network** allows you to see and be seen by other computers and share devices and the connection. By selecting this, you can choose what to share with others (such as pictures or documents).

   • **Work Network** is a more private setting with less automatic sharing of items with others.

   • **Public Network** is the most secure setting and won't allow you to set up a group or access other computers on the network.

 Your computer uses the default connection anytime you click a link to an online location or open your browser. However, you can still manually open any connection by opening the Network and Internet window, clicking the Connect to a Network link, right-clicking any connection, and choosing Connect.

Figure 6-9: The Network and Sharing Center window

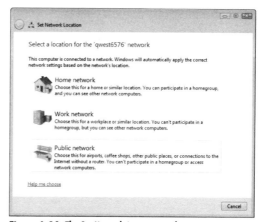

Figure 6-10: The Set Network Location window

 Why would you need to change a connection? If you travel with a laptop, you may want to change your default connection from your home network to a wireless connection provided at an airport or hotel, for example. Or, you may use one connection at home and one at the office.

Remove an Internet Connection

1. Choose Start➪Control Panel➪Network and Internet.

2. In the resulting window, click the Network and Sharing Center link.

3. In the resulting window (see Figure 6-11), click the Manage Wireless Networks link.

4. In the Manage Wireless Networks window (see Figure 6-12), right-click the connection and then click Remove Network. The connection name is removed from the network connections list.

Even if you no longer need a connection, as long as you don't click it, there's no harm in leaving it in your connections list. However, somebody else using your computer may be unsure as to which connection to activate, and your list of connections will be more cluttered if you don't get rid of old connections.

Figure 6-11: The Network and Sharing Center window

Figure 6-12: The Manage Wireless Networks window

Browsing the Web with Internet Explorer

To drive around the Internet superhighway, you need a good vehicle. A *browser*, such as Internet Explorer (IE), is a program that you can use to get around the Internet.

IE is built into Windows because it's made by Microsoft, so the Microsoft folks can put it anywhere they like. You can download other browsers, such as Mozilla Firefox, for free.

In this chapter, you discover the ins and outs of using Internet Explorer. By using IE you can

- **Navigate the Web.** Use the IE navigation features to jump from one site to another, go back to places you've been (via the Favorites and History features), and search for new places to visit.

- **Download files to your computer or print hard copies.** When you find what you want online, such as a graphic image or a free software program, you might want to save it to your computer for future use. Do you need a hard copy of what you've found? Just use the Print feature of IE.

- **Protect yourself.** The Internet is a bit dangerous — a place where some people try to get at your private information and make nefarious use of it. IE provides privacy settings and special features to control the use of *cookies* (small files that folks who run Web sites insert on your hard drive to help them track your online activities). You can use the Content Advisor to limit the online locations that your computer can visit and explore some safety features new to Internet Explorer 8: InPrivate Filtering and Blocking and the SmartScreen Filter.

Get ready to . . .

Navigate the Web

1. Open IE by clicking the Internet Explorer icon in the Quick Access area of the Windows taskbar.

2. Enter a Web site address in the Address bar, as shown in Figure 7-1 (`www.ilookbothways.com` is my company's Web site), and then press Enter.

3. On the resulting Web site, click a *link* (short for *hyperlink;* a link takes you to another online page or document), display another page on the site using navigation tools on the page (such as the Learn About Safety and Education buttons on the page in Figure 7-1), or enter another address in the Address bar to proceed to another page.

    A link can be an icon or text. A text link is identifiable by colored text, usually blue. After you click a link, it usually changes to another color, such as purple, to show that it's been followed.

4. Click the Back button to move back to the first page that you visited. Click the Forward button to go forward to the second page that you visited.

5. Click the down arrow at the far right of the Address bar to display a list of sites that you've visited recently, as shown in Figure 7-2. Click a site in this list to go there.

    The Refresh and Stop buttons on the right end of the Address bar are useful for navigating sites. Clicking the Refresh button redisplays the current page. This is especially useful if a page updates information frequently, such as on a stock market site. You can also use the Refresh button if a page doesn't load correctly; it might load correctly when refreshed. Clicking the Stop button stops a page that's loading. So, if you made a mistake entering the address or if the page is taking longer than you want to load, click the Stop button to halt the process.

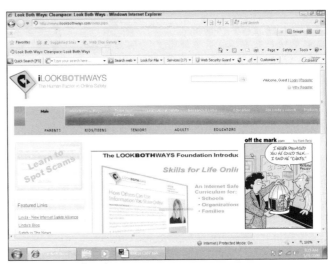

Figure 7-1: My Web site home page

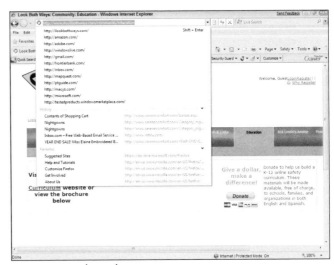

Figure 7-2: Recently visited sites

Search the Web

1. Open IE and click in the Search pane on the toolbar.

2. Enter a search term in the text box and then click Search. In this example, I use Windows Live Search as the search engine.

3. In the search results that appear (see Figure 7-3), click a link to go to that Web page. If you don't see the link that you need, click and drag the scroll bar to view more results.

4. Click the Options link at the top of the Search window to change Search settings.

5. In the resulting Options dialog box, as shown in Figure 7-4, select options for one of the following and then click Save Settings to apply it:

   • **SafeSearch:** These options let you set filtering of search results at three levels: Strict, Moderate, and Off.

   • **Location:** Enter your geographical location to have search results returned that are relevant to where you live.

   • **Display:** Here you can set the language to be used in displayed search results.

   • **Results:** Select one of these options to determine whether results are opened in the current browser window or whether Windows Live opens a new browser window.

   • **Search Suggestions:** With this feature on, suggested search terms appear as you type in the Search field based on similar searches.

   • **Search Language:** Choose a language to search only pages written in that language.

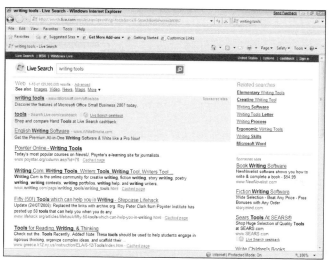

Figure 7-3: Search results displayed in Windows Live Search

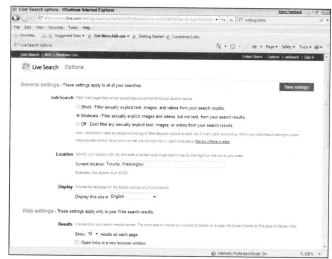

Figure 7-4: The Options dialog box

Find Content on a Web Page

1. With IE open and the Web page that you want to search displayed, click the arrow on the Search box, and choose Find on This Page.

2. In the resulting Find toolbar that appears on the active tab, as shown in Figure 7-5, enter the word that you want to search for. As you type, all instances of the word on the page are highlighted. Click the Options button and use the following options to narrow your results:

   - **Match Whole Word Only:** Select this option if you want to find only the whole word (for example, if you enter **elect** and want to find only *elect* and not *electron* or *electronics*).

   - **Match Case:** Select this option if you want to match the case (for example, if you enter **Catholic** and want to find only the always-capitalized religion and not the adjective *catholic*).

3. Click the Next button and you move from one high-lighted instance of the word to the next (see Figure 7-6). If you want to move to a previous instance, click the Previous button.

4. When you're done searching, click the Close button on the left side of the Find toolbar.

 Many Web sites have a Search This Site feature that allows you to search not only the displayed Web page but all Web pages on a Web site, or search by department or category of item in an online store. Look for a Search text box and make sure that it searches the site — and not the entire Internet.

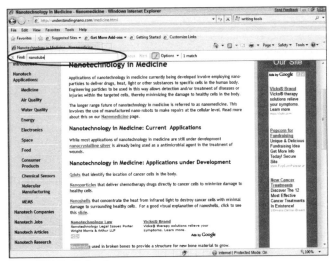

Figure 7-5: The Find toolbar

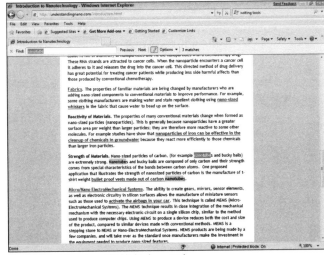

Figure 7-6: A found word highlighted on a Web page

Set Up a Home Page

1. Open IE and choose Tools➪Internet Options.

2. In the resulting Internet Options dialog box, on the General tab, enter a Web site address to use as your home page, as shown in Figure 7-7, and then click OK. Note that you can enter several home pages that will appear on different tabs every time you open IE, as shown in Figure 7-8.

   Alternatively, click one of the following preset option buttons, as shown in Figure 7-7:

   - **Use Current:** Sets whatever page is currently displayed in the browser window as your home page.

   - **Use Default:** This setting sends you to the MSN Web page.

   - **Use Blank:** If you're a minimalist, this setting is for you. No Web page displays; you just see a blank area.

3. Click the Home button on the IE toolbar (it looks like a little house) to go to your home page.

 If you want to have more than one home page, you can create multiple home page tabs that will display when you click the Home button. Click the arrow on the Home button and choose Add or Change Home Page. In the Add or Change Home Page dialog box that appears, click the Add This Webpage to Your Home Page Tabs radio button and then click Yes. Display other sites and repeat this procedure for all the home page tabs you want.

 To remove a home page you have set up, click the arrow on the Home button and choose Remove and then choose a particular home page, or choose Remove All from the submenu that appears.

Figure 7-7: The Internet Options dialog box

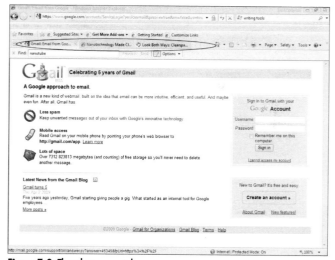

Figure 7-8: Three home page tabs

Add a Web Site to Favorites

1. Open IE, enter the URL (Uniform Resource Locator) of a Web site that you want to add to your Favorites list, and then press Enter.

2. Click the Favorites button to display the Favorites pane and then click the Add to Favorites button.

3. In the resulting Add a Favorite dialog box, shown in Figure 7-9, modify the name of the Favorite listing to something easily recognizable. If you wish, choose another folder or create a folder to store the Favorite in.

4. Click Add to add the site.

5. Click the Favorites button to display the Favorites Center, and then click the name of the site from the list that's displayed (see Figure 7-10) to go to that site.

Regularly cleaning out your Favorites list is a good idea — after all, do you really need the sites that you used to plan last year's vacation? With the Favorites Center displayed, right-click any item and then choose Delete or Rename to modify the favorite listing.

You can keep the Favorites Center as a side pane in Internet Explorer by displaying it and then clicking the Pin the Favorites Center button (it has a left-facing green arrow on it and is located in the top-right corner of the pane).

Figure 7-9: The Add a Favorite dialog box

Figure 7-10: Favorite Web sites displayed in the Favorites pane

Organize Favorites

1. With Internet Explorer open, click the Favorites button to open the Favorites pane. Click the arrow on the right of the Add to Favorites button and then choose Organize Favorites.

2. In the resulting Organize Favorites dialog box (see Figure 7-11), click the New Folder button, or select a site or folder and then click the Move, Rename, or Delete buttons to organize your favorites.

3. After you finish organizing your Favorites, click Close.

 These steps provide a handy way to manage several sites or folders, but you can also organize favorite sites one by one by using the Favorites pane. (You display the Favorites pane by clicking the Favorites button.) Right-click any favorite site listed in the pane and choose a command: Create New Folder, Rename, or Delete, for example.

Figure 7-11: The Organize Favorites dialog box

 If you create new folders in the earlier steps, you'll have to manually transfer files into those folders or select the files when adding Favorites. To do this, just display the Favorites Center and click and drag Internet shortcuts listed there on top of folders.

Use Suggested Sites

1. To have Internet Explorer suggest sites you might like that are related to the currently displayed site, click the Tools button and choose Suggested Sites (a check mark appears next to it, as shown in Figure 7-12). If this is the first time you've activated the feature, a message may appear asking you to subscribe to links to enable your computer to search for updates at any time.

2. Click the Suggested Sites button on the Favorites toolbar. (If the toolbar isn't displayed, right-click the toolbar area and choose Favorites Bar.) A list of suggested sites appears in a pop-up window (see Figure 7-13).

3. Click a site to display its URL.

 Suggested Sites uses your browsing history to come up with suggestions, so when you first activate it, it may take a little while before it comes up with useful suggestions.

Figure 7-12: Activating Suggested Sites

Figure 7-13: The Suggested Sites pane

Work with Tabs

1. With Internet Explorer open, click New Tab (the smallest tab on the far right of the tabs).

2. When the new tab appears, which displays some information about tabs (see Figure 7-14), enter a URL in the Address bar. The URL opens in that tab. You can then click other tabs to switch among sites.

3. Click the Quicktabs button (it consists of four little squares on the far left of the tabs) to display a thumbnail of all open tabs (see Figure 7-15), or click the Tab List button (the arrow to the right of the Quicktabs button) to display a text list of tabs.

4. Close an active tab by clicking the Close button on the right.

 A *tab* is a sort of window you can use to view any number of sites. You don't have to create a new tab to go to another site. Having the ability to keep a few tabs open at a time means you can more quickly switch among two or more sites without navigating back and forth either with the Previous or Next button or by entering URLs. You can also create more than one Home Page tab that can appear every time you open IE. See the earlier task "Set Up a Home Page" for more about this.

 You can also press Ctrl+T to open a new tab in Internet Explorer. If you want to keep one tab open and close all others, right-click the tab you want to keep open and choose Close Other Tabs.

Figure 7-14: A newly created tab

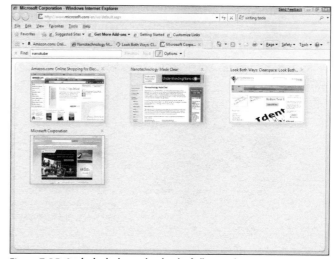

Figure 7-15: Quicktabs displaying thumbnails of all open tabs

View Your Browsing History

1. Click the Favorites button and then click History to display the History pane (see Figure 7-16).

2. Click the down arrow on the History button (see Figure 7-17) and select a sort method:

   • **By Date:** Sort Favorites by date visited.

   • **By Site:** Sort alphabetically by site name.

   • **By Most Visited:** Sort with the sites visited most on top and those visited least at the bottom of the list.

   • **By Order Visited Today:** Sort by the order in which you visited sites today.

3. In the History pane, you can click a site to go to it. The History pane closes unless you have it pinned.

 You can also click the arrow on the right of the Address bar to display sites you've visited.

 Choose Search History on the History menu to display a search box you can use to search for sites you've visited.

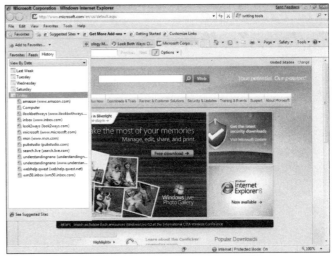

Figure 7-16: The History pane

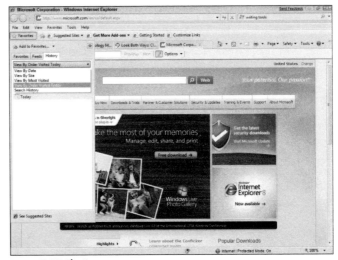

Figure 7-17: The History sort menu

Customize the Internet Explorer Toolbar

1. Open IE.

2. Choose Tools⇨Toolbars⇨Customize. The Customize Toolbar dialog box (as shown in Figure 7-18) appears.

3. Click a tool on the left and then click the Add button to add it to the toolbar.

4. Click a tool on the right and then click the Remove button to remove it from the toolbar.

5. When you're finished, click Close to save your new toolbar settings. The new tools appear; click the double-arrow button on the right of the toolbar to display any tools that IE can't fit onscreen (see Figure 7-19).

 You can use the Move Up and Move Down buttons in the Customize Toolbar dialog box to rearrange the order in which tools appear on the toolbar. To reset the toolbar to defaults, click the Reset button in that same dialog box.

 If you want to add some space between tools on the toolbar so it's easier to see, click the Separator item in the Available Toolbar Buttons list and add it before or after a tool button.

Figure 7-18: The Customize Toolbar dialog box

Figure 7-19: Display any additional tools by clicking the button on the right of the toolbar

Download Files

1. Open a Web site that contains downloadable files. Typically Web sites offer a Download button or a link that initiates a file download.

2. Click the appropriate link to proceed. Windows might display a dialog box asking your permission to proceed with the download; click Yes.

3. In the resulting File Download dialog box, as shown in Figure 7-20, choose an option:

   - **Click Run to download to a temporary folder.** You can run an installation program for software, for example. However, beware: If you run a program directly from the Internet, you could be introducing dangerous viruses to your system. You might want to set up an antivirus program to scan files before downloading them.

   - **Click Save to save the file to your hard drive.** In the Save As dialog box, select the folder on your computer or removable storage media (a USB Flash drive, for example) where you want to save the file. If you're downloading software, you need to locate the downloaded file and click it to run the installation.

Figure 7-20: The File Download dialog box

 If you're worried that a particular file might be unsafe to download (for example, if it's from an unknown source and, being an executable file type, could contain a virus), click Cancel in the File Download dialog box.

 If a particular file will take a long time to download (some can take 20 minutes or more), you may have to babysit it. If your computer goes into standby, it could pause the download. If your computer automatically downloads Windows updates, it may cause your computer to restart automatically as well, cancelling or halting your download. Check in periodically to keep things moving along.

Turn on InPrivate Browsing and Blocking

1. InPrivate Browsing is a new feature that stops IE from saving information about your browsing session, such as cookies and your browsing history. InPrivate Blocking allows you to block or allow sites that are automatically collecting information about your browsing habits. To turn on InPrivate features, open IE.

2. Click the Safety button and choose InPrivate Browsing to turn on that feature. The window shown in Figure 7-21 appears.

3. Click the Safety button and choose InPrivate Blocking; the dialog box shown in Figure 7-22 appears. Choose one of the following settings:

   - **Automatically Block** blocks any site that uses content from other sites you've visited.

   - **Manually Block** allows you to open the InPrivate Blocking Settings dialog box and use the Allow and Block buttons to select which sites to allow and which to block.

4. Click OK to save your settings. When you browse a bit and then reopen the InPrivate Blocking Settings dialog box (Safety⇨InPrivate Block), you see blocked and allowed sites listed.

 If you don't want to use InPrivate Browsing but want to periodically clear your browsing history manually, with IE open, you can press Ctrl+Shift+Delete to do so.

Figure 7-21: The window noting that InPrivate Browsing has been turned on

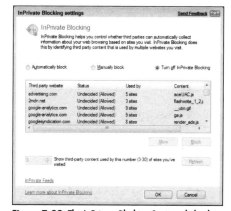

Figure 7-22: The InPrivate Blocking Settings dialog box

Use SmartScreen Filter

1. SmartScreen Filter lets you check Web sites that have been reported to Microsoft as generating phishing scams or downloading malware to your computer. To turn on SmartScreen Filter, click the Safety button and then choose SmartScreen Filter➪Turn On SmartScreen Filter.

2. To use SmartScreen Filter, go to a Web site you want to check. Click the Safety button and choose SmartScreen Filter➪Check This Website.

3. The SmartScreen Filter window appears (see Figure 7-23), indicating whether it found any threats. Click OK to close the message.

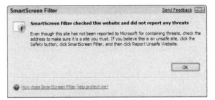

Figure 7-23: Checking a Web site with SmartScreen Filter

 When turned on, SmartScreen Filter automatically checks Web sites and generates a message if you visit one that has reported problems. However, that information gets updated only periodically, so if you have concerns about a particular site, use the procedure given here to check the latest information about the Web site.

Change Privacy Settings

1. With IE open, choose Tools⇨Internet Options and click the Privacy tab, as shown in Figure 7-24.

2. Click the slider and drag it up or down to make different levels of security settings.

3. Read the choices and select a setting that suits you.

4. Click the Sites button to specify sites to always or never allow the use of cookies. In the resulting Per Site Privacy Actions dialog box (as shown in Figure 7-25), enter a site in the Address of Website box and click either Block or Allow.

5. Click OK twice to save your new settings.

 The default setting, Medium, is probably a good bet for most people. To restore the default setting, click the Default button in the Internet Options dialog box Privacy tab or use the slider to move back to Medium.

 You can also use Pop-Up Blocker settings on the Privacy tab to specify which pop-up windows to allow or block. Just click the Settings button, enter a Web site name, and then click Add to allow pop-ups.

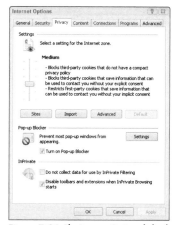

Figure 7-24: The Internet Options dialog box, Privacy tab

Figure 7-25: The Per Site Privacy Actions dialog box

Enable the Content Advisor

1. With IE open, choose Tools⇨Internet Options.

2. In the resulting Internet Options dialog box, click the Content tab to display it.

3. Click the Enable button. (*Note:* If you don't see an Enable button but see Disable and Settings buttons instead, Content Advisor is already enabled. Click the Settings button to see the options and make changes if you wish.)

4. On the Ratings tab of the Content Advisor dialog box (see Figure 7-26), click one of the categories (such as Depiction of Drug Use) and then move the slider to use one of three site-screening settings: None, Limited, or Unrestricted.

5. Repeat Step 4 for each of the categories.

6. Click the Approved Sites tab (see Figure 7-27) and enter the name of a specific site that you want to control access to. Then click Always or Never.

   - **Always** allows users to view the site, even if it's included in the Content Advisor screening level you've set.

   - **Never** means that nobody can visit the site even if it's acceptable to Content Advisor.

7. When you finish making your settings, click OK twice to save them.

 If you want to view sites that you don't want others to see, you can do that, too. On the General tab of the Content Advisor dialog box, make sure that the Supervisor Can Type a Password to Allow Viewers to View Restricted Content check box is selected and then click Create Password. In the dialog box that appears, enter the password, confirm it, and then enter a hint and click OK. Now if you're logged on as the system administrator, you can get to any restricted site by using this password.

Figure 7-26: The Ratings tab of the Content Advisor dialog box

Figure 7-27: The Approved Sites tab of the Content Advisor

 To find rating systems that various organizations have created and apply them to Internet Explorer, click the Rating Systems button on the General tab. Here you can choose a system already shown there. Or, click Add; then, in the resulting Open Ratings System File dialog box, choose another system to apply.

View RSS Feeds

1. *RSS (Really Simple Syndication)* is a feature you can use to have news and other frequently updated information sent to you. Click the Favorites button; then click the Feeds tab to display a list of recently displayed RSS feeds (see Figure 7-28).

2. Click a feed to display it (see Figure 7-29).

3. You can also click the View Feeds on This Page button on the toolbar to view any active feeds listed on the currently displayed page.

 The View Feeds on This Page button is grayed out when no RSS feeds are on the current page, and it turns red when feeds are present.

 Though Internet Explorer has an RSS feed reader built in, you can explore other feed readers. Just type **RSS feeds** into Internet Explorer's Search box to find more information and listings of readers and RSS feed sites.

Figure 7-28: The RSS Feeds pane

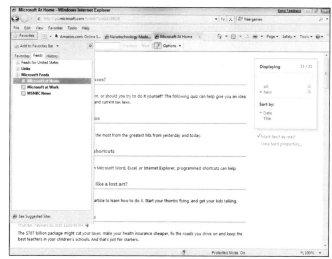

Figure 7-29: An RSS Feed site

Print a Web Page

1. If a Web page includes a link or a button to print or display a print version of a page, click that and follow the instructions.

2. If the page doesn't include a link for printing, click the Print button on the IE toolbar.

3. In the resulting Print dialog box, decide how much of the document you want to print and then select one of the options in the Page Range area, as shown in Figure 7-30.

     Note that choosing Current Page or entering page numbers in the Pages text box of the Print dialog box doesn't mean much when printing a Web page — the whole document might print because Web pages aren't divided into pages like word processing documents are.

4. Click the up arrow in the Number of Copies text box to print multiple copies. If you want multiple copies collated, select the Collate check box.

5. After you adjust all settings you need, click Print.

Figure 7-30: The Print dialog box

Exchanging E-Mail with Windows Live Mail

*O*nce upon a time, people chatted around the water cooler or over lunch, but that's all changed now. Now the place to spend your time communicating is online.

Although instant messaging from your cellphone is all the rage, e-mail is still the cornerstone of online communication. You've probably sent an e-mail (unless you were brought up by wolves in the forest), but you might not be familiar with the ins and outs of using *Windows Live Mail* (or just *Windows Mail*), a Microsoft e-mail program. You can download Windows Live Mail to your computer (go to www.download.live.com to do so) and access it from your Start menu, or you can simply log onto the Windows Live site from any computer to use all its features (which is the method I describe in the tasks in this chapter).

To make your e-mailing life easy, this chapter takes a look at these tasks:

➡ **Receive, send, and forward messages.** Deal with the ins and outs of receiving and sending e-mail. Use the formatting tools that Windows Mail provides to make your messages more attractive and readable.

➡ **Add information to the Address Book.** You can quickly and easily manage your contacts as well as organize the messages you save in e-mail folders.

➡ **Set up the layout of all Windows Mail features.** Use the Folder bar and Layout features to create the most efficient workspace.

➡ **Manage your e-mail account.** Set up an e-mail account, and then create, modify, and add rules for your account to operate by.

Get ready to . . .

Open Windows Live Mail and Receive Messages

1. Go to the Windows Live home page using your browser (www.windowslive.com).

2. Windows opens your default browser and displays the Windows Live sign-in window shown in Figure 8-1. If you need to start a new account at this point, click the Sign Up button and go through the sign-up procedure.

3. Click the Sign in to Windows Live button and enter your password in the field that appears, and then click the Sign In button to sign in. Windows Live automatically sends and receives all messages.

4. Click the Mail link at the top of the page to view your Inbox (see Figure 8-2). New messages sport a small closed envelope icon; those with attachments have a paper clip icon as well.

 To organize messages in the Inbox, click the Sort By button and choose any of the categories, such as From (to sort the messages alphabetically by sender), Subject, Date, and so on.

 If your mail doesn't come through, it's probably because your e-mail provider's servers are experiencing technical problems. Just wait a little while. If you still can't get mail (and you know you should have received some by now), contact your e-mail provider to find out what the problem is and when it will be fixed.

 If an e-mail has a little exclamation point to the left of it in your Inbox, somebody has flagged it as urgent. It's usually best to check those e-mails first!

Figure 8-1: The Windows Live sign-in screen

Figure 8-2: The Windows Live Inbox

Create and Send E-Mail

1. Go to the Windows Live home page using your browser (www.windowslive.com).

2. Sign in and then click the Mail button on the Windows Live screen to go to your Inbox.

3. Click the New button to create a new, blank e-mail form (see Figure 8-3).

4. Type the e-mail address of the recipient(s) in the To field text box. If you want to send a copy of the message, click the Show Cc & Bcc link and enter the address(es) in the Cc or Bcc field text box(es).

5. Click in the Subject field text box and type a concise yet descriptive subject.

6. Click in the message window and type your message (see Figure 8-4).

 Don't press Enter at the end of a line when typing a message. Windows Mail has an automatic text wrap feature that does this for you. Do be concise. If you have lots to say, consider sending a letter by snail mail or overnight delivery. Most people tire of reading text onscreen after a short while.

 Keep e-mail etiquette in mind while you type. For example, don't type in ALL CAPITAL LETTERS. This is called *shouting,* which is considered rude. Do be polite even if you're really, really angry. Your message could be forwarded to just about anybody, just about anywhere, and you don't want to get a reputation as a hothead.

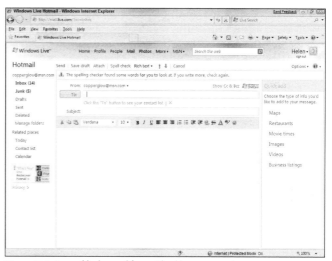

Figure 8-3: A new, blank e-mail form with addresses entered

Figure 8-4: A message typed and ready to go

7. When you finish typing your message, check your spelling (unless you're the regional state spelling champ). Click the Spell Check button, and Windows Live automatically checks spelling and places a red wavy line under questionable words (see Figure 8-5). Correct any errors. If you add more text to your message and want to check the new text for spelling, click the Spell Check button again.

8. Click the Send button. A message appears like the one in Figure 8-6 telling you the message is on its way!

 If the message is really urgent, you might also click the High Importance button (it looks like a red exclamation point) to add a bright red exclamation mark to the message header to alert the recipient. Click the Low Importance button (it looks like a blue downward-pointing arrow) to return the priority to Low.

 Remember that when creating an e-mail, you can address it to a stored address by using the Address Book feature. Click the To button, and your Address Book appears. You can then select your contact(s) from there. Windows Mail also allows you to just begin to type a stored contact in an address field (To or Cc), and it fills in likely options while you type. When it fills in the correct name, just press Enter to select it.

Figure 8-5: The Spell Check feature at work

Figure 8-6: Confirmation that a message was sent

Send an Attachment

1. Go to www.windowslive.com, sign in, and click Mail. Click New to create a new e-mail message, address it, and enter a subject.

2. Click the Attach button.

3. The Choose File to Upload dialog box appears (see Figure 8-7). Locate the file that you want and then click Open.

4. The name of the attached file appears in the Attach field text box (see Figure 8-8). You can click the Attach button again and repeat Step 3 as many times as you like to add additional attachments.

5. Click the Send button to send the message and attachment.

 You can attach as many files as you like to a single e-mail by repeating steps in this task. Your only limitation is size. Various e-mail programs have different limitations on the size of attachments. If you attach several documents and your e-mail fails to get sent, just send a few e-mails and spread the attachments out among them.

Figure 8-7: The Choose File to Upload box

Figure 8-8: The Attach field showing an attached file

Read a Message

1. Click an e-mail message in your Inbox or double-click it to open it in a larger window. Unread messages sport an unopened envelope icon to the left of the message subject.

2. If the message is long, use the scroll bars in the message window to scroll down through the message and read it.

3. If the message has an attachment, it shows a paper clip symbol when the message is closed in your Inbox (see Figure 8-9). To open an attachment, click it.

4. In the File Download dialog box (see Figure 8-10), click the Open button to open the file with the suggested program. The attachment opens in whatever program is associated with it (such as the Windows Picture and Fax Viewer for a graphics file) or the program it was created in (such as Word for Windows).

 If you'd rather save an attachment to a storage disk or your hard drive, click the Save button in Step 4, choose the location to save the file to, and then click Save.

Figure 8-9: A newly received e-mail message with attachment

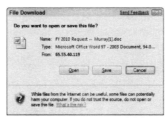

Figure 8-10: The File Download dialog box

Reply to a Message

1. Open the message you want to reply to and then select one of the following reply options, as shown in Figure 8-11:

   • **Reply:** Send the reply to only the author.

   • **Reply All:** Send a reply to the author as well as everyone who received the original message.

2. In the resulting e-mail form (see Figure 8-12), enter any additional recipient(s) in the To and/or Cc or Bcc text boxes, and type your message in the message window area.

3. Click the Send button to send the reply.

 If you don't want to include the original message in your reply, choose Tools➪Options and click the Send tab. Deselect the Include Message in Reply check box and then click OK.

Figure 8-11: The Reply and Reply All options

Figure 8-12: A reply message

Forward E-Mail

1. Open the e-mail message that you want to forward.

2. Click the Forward button on the toolbar.

3. In the message that appears with *FW:* added to the beginning of the subject line, enter a new recipient(s) in the To and/or Cc and Bcc fields, and then enter any message that you want to include in the message window area, as shown in the example in Figure 8-13.

4. Click Send to forward the message.

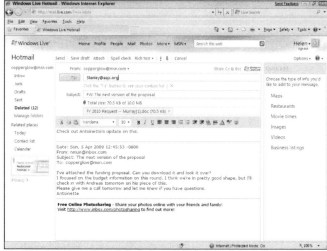

Figure 8-13: A message ready to be forwarded

Create and Add a Signature

1. Choose Options⇨More Options to open the Options window. Click the Personal E-mail Signature link (under Customize Your Mail) (see Figure 8-14).

2. In the Personal E-mail Signature form that opens (see Figure 8-15), type your signature. Use the tools on the toolbar to change the text formatting. For example, you can change the font or font size, or apply effects, such as Bold or Italic.

3. Click Save to save the signature.

 If you have a Web site and want to include a link to it in your signature, click the Insert Hyperlink tool button (it looks like a little blue globe with chain links in front of it) in the toolbar shown in Figure 8-15. Enter the address in the field text box that appears and then click OK.

 Remember that if you attach your signature to every outgoing e-mail including e-mail replies, whoever you communicate with will get the information provided there. Consider issues of identity theft before you provide your address, phone number, and other personal information to all and sundry.

Figure 8-14: The Options window

Figure 8-15: The Personal E-mail Signature form

Format E-Mail Messages

1. Create a new e-mail message or open a message and click Reply, Reply All, or Forward.

2. Enter text, and then select the text that you want to format (see Figure 8-16).

3. Use any of the following options to make changes to the font. (See the toolbar containing these tools in Figure 8-17.)

   - **Font drop-down list:** Choose an option from the drop-down list to apply it to the text.

   - **Font Size drop-down list:** Change the font size here.

   - **Bold, Italic, or Underline buttons:** Apply styles to selected text.

   - **Align Left, Justify Center, Align Right buttons:** Adjust the alignment.

   - **Formatting Numbers or Formatting Bullets buttons:** Apply numbering order to lists or precede each item with a round bullet.

   - **Increase Indentation or Decrease Indentation button:** Indent that paragraph to the right or move (decrease) it to the left.

   - **Insert Hyperlink button:** Use this to insert a hyperlink to another Web site or document.

   - **Insert Horizontal Rule button:** Insert a line dividing the signature from the message body.

   - **Font Color button:** Display a color palette and click a color to apply it to selected text.

   - **Background Color button:** Add color to the background of the message.

Figure 8-16: Text selected for formatting

Figure 8-17: The formatting toolbar

Add a Theme

1. You can modify the appearance of Windows Live Mail by applying a theme. Choose Options➪More Themes.

2. In the Themes dialog box that appears (see Figure 8-18), click a theme from the list.

3. Click Save to apply the stationery to Windows Live Mail, and click the Mail link to return to your Inbox sporting the new look (see Figure 8-19).

> If you're the visual type, know that you can also insert a picture in an e-mail message. With a new e-mail form open, click the Images item in the Quick Add pane to the right. Enter a search term in the Search field text box to find an image online and then click any image result to insert it in your e-mail. You can also use Quick Add to add a map, movie time, video, business listing, or restaurant information.

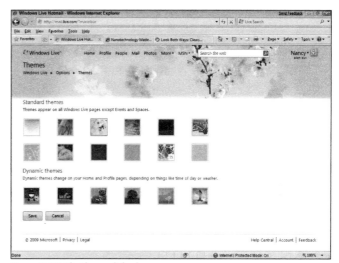

Figure 8-18: The Themes dialog box

Figure 8-19: A theme applied to Windows Live Mail

Add People to the Contact List

1. In the Windows Live Mail main window, click the Contact List link in the left pane to open the People window, as shown in Figure 8-20.

2. To create a new contact, click the New button.

3. In the resulting Contact dialog box, as shown in Figure 8-21, enter contact information:

   - **Name and e-mail:** Enter the person's first and last name. (This is the only information you must enter to create a contact.)

   - **Personal Information:** Enter the person's e-mail address, home and mobile phone numbers, and home address.

   - **Business Information:** Enter information about the company that the person works for as well as his work e-mail, phone, fax, and address.

   - **Other Information:** Enter any other e-mail, phone, Web site, or birthday information for the person.

4. Click Save to save your new contact information and then click Mail to return to your Inbox.

  You can search contacts by clicking People in the Mail window and entering search text in the Search Your Contact List field. You can also click the letters listed across the top of the Contacts window to look for people whose last names begin with that letter.

Figure 8-20: The People window showing contacts starting with "P"

Figure 8-21: The Contact dialog box

Customize the Reading Pane Layout

1. Choose Options⇨More Options to open the Options window.

2. Click Reading Pane Settings (under Customize Your Mail). Select various options in the Reading Pane Settings dialog box, as shown in Figure 8-22, to modify where the reading pane appears and when to show messages in the reading pane.

3. Click Save to save your reading pane settings.

Create Message Folders

1. Choose the Manage Folders link near the bottom of the folders list within the Inbox in the left pane to open the Manage Folders window, shown in Figure 8-23.

2. Click New.

3. In the New Folder dialog box, enter a folder name and click Save.

4. Click Mail to return to your Inbox.

 If you want to remove or rename a folder, you can use the tools in the Manage Folders window shown in Figure 8-23 to do so.

Figure 8-22: The Reading Pane Settings dialog box

Figure 8-23: The Manage Folders window

Organize Messages in Folders

1. To move a message in your Inbox into a folder, select the check box in front of the message and choose Move To⇨*[Folder Name]* (see Figure 8-24).

2. To move a message between folders, with a folder (such as the Inbox) displayed, click a message and then drag it into another folder in the Folders list.

3. To delete a message in a folder, click the folder name to open it and select the check box in front of the message. Click Delete.

 If you want to mark a message as Junk mail so that Windows Live Mail puts any message from that sender in the Junk folder going forward, select the check box in front of the message and then click Junk.

Figure 8-24: Select a message by clicking the check box

Working Remotely

*W*e live in a hurry-up-and-go society. Gone are the days when you could sit back during your flight from Des Moines to Chicago and take a snooze. These days, people do as much work in the air and on the road as in cubicles and offices.

Windows 7 hasn't left the road warrior behind: It offers several features that help keep you in touch and help you connect your Windows computer wirelessly and get your work done.

Windows 7 remote control features include

➡ Power management tools — *power plans* — for laptops to make sure that you don't run out of juice at an all-important moment

➡ The ability to connect to a wireless network, such as the kind you find in airports, restaurants, and hotels

➡ Features to help you set up and give presentations on the road

Chapter 9

Get ready to . . .

Create a Power Plan for a Laptop

1. Choose Start➪Control Panel➪System and Security, and then click the Power Options link.

2. In the Select a Power Plan window, as shown in Figure 9-1, select a scheme.

3. To change settings, click the Change Plan Settings link next to any power plan. In the window that displays (see Figure 9-2), click the arrow and choose another setting for the length of inactivity time before the display dims or shuts off to save power.

4. Click the Save Changes button to save the settings, and then click the Close button to close the Control Panel.

 In the window for changing plan settings, you can click the Change Advanced Power Settings link to modify settings, such as requiring a password to wake up your computer, when to turn off your hard disk, or when to automatically go into hibernation mode.

 Other power plans are available. From the Power Plan window, click the arrow to the right of Show Additional Plans. Note that Windows recommends the Balanced plan. This provides a balance of performance and energy savings that works when you use your laptop at home or on a short outing. For longer trips, the Power Saver and Power4Gear Battery Saving plans are best and will provide the longest battery life.

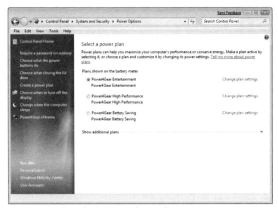

Figure 9-1: The Select a Power Plan window

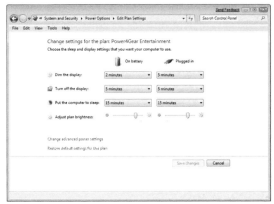

Figure 9-2: Changing Power Plan settings

Create a Custom Power Plan

1. Choose Start⇨Control Panel⇨System and Security, and then click the Power Options link.

2. In the Power Options window, click the Create a Power Plan link in the left panel.

3. In the Create a Power Plan window (see Figure 9-3), select the plan that's closest to what you want to create, enter the name for your plan in the Plan Name field, and then click Next.

4. In the Edit Plan Settings window that appears (see Figure 9-4), click the arrow to display a drop-down list of timings for dimming or turning off the display and then choose a new setting. You can also use the slider to adjust screen brightness to save power, if you wish.

5. Click the Create button to add the plan to your list of power plans.

 If you create a plan, no Energy Savings or Performance ratings are next to it in the plan list. Also, if you make changes to an existing plan, those ratings don't change. If somebody else will use the computer, either let him know about this or reset the plans to default to avoid confusion. (In the Change Plan Settings window, select Restore Default Settings for This Plan.)

Figure 9-3: The Create a Power Plan window

Figure 9-4: The Edit Plan Settings window

Connect to a Wireless Network

1. If your computer is enabled with a network card, it can connect wirelessly with private or public networks to go online. Choose Start⇨Control Panel⇨Network and Internet.

2. Click Connect to a Network. The Connect to a Network window appears (see Figure 9-5).

3. Click a network to select it and then click Connect. If the network is private and secure, you're asked to enter a code to access it. If it's a public network, such as in an airport or a hotel, Windows 7 checks the connection and connects you.

Figure 9-5: The Connect to a Network window

Modify Display Brightness to Save Power

1. Adjusting your display to a lower brightness setting can help you save power when you're on the road. Choose Start⇨Control Panel and click Adjust Commonly Used Mobility Settings under the Hardware and Sound option.

2. In the Windows Mobility Center dialog box, as shown in Figure 9-6, click and drag the Brightness slider left or right to change the setting.

3. Click the Close button to close the Mobility Center.

 Some settings shown in Figure 9-6 may not appear on your computer if you don't have the corresponding feature; for example, if your computer doesn't have wireless capability, the Turn Wireless On item might not be included.

Figure 9-6: The Windows Mobility Center

 The Mobility Center is new in Windows 7 and gives you one location to make settings that might affect your battery power or wireless connections. If you're on the road a lot, it's useful to know what's available in the Center and that you can access more options for each setting in it by clicking an icon.

Check Your Battery Status

1. With the Windows system tray displayed, as shown in Figure 9-7, hover your mouse over the Battery icon. The percentage of battery power and remaining hours of usage are displayed.

2. For more details, click the Battery icon. A window appears (see Figure 9-8). Note that the contents of this window may vary based on your computer manufacturer's settings.

3. From this window, you can

    • Switch to a different power plan

    • Adjust screen brightness to save power

    • Access more power options

4. Click anywhere outside the Battery window to close it.

Figure 9-7: The Battery icon on the taskbar

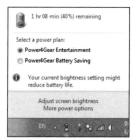

Figure 9-8: The Battery window

 You can also access information about your battery through the Windows Mobility Center. Go to the Control Panel and click the Adjust Commonly Used Mobility Settings link to display the Center.

If you want the maximum battery power, consider buying a netbook. These compact computers are not only lightweight (2–3 pounds), but some have battery lives of more than nine hours.

Connect to a Projector

1. Connect a projector device to your computer (this is done by plugging a VGA or DVI cable into the video port on your computer). Choose Start⇨Control Panel and click the Connect to a Projector link in the Hardware and Sound settings.

2. In the window that appears (see Figure 9-9), click one of four settings:

   • **Show Desktop Only on Computer Display** uses your current display (on a laptop that's the display in the lid).

   • **Duplicate Desktop on Projector** shows your desktop on both your current display and a connected projector.

   • **Extend Desktop to Projector** splits the image between the two displays.

   • **Show Desktop Only on Projector** turns off the current display and displays the desktop only on the projector.

3. When you click a setting, the Projector settings window closes and the setting takes effect.

Figure 9-9: The Connect to a Projector window

 A handy shortcut to connect to a projector is to press Ctrl+⊞+P. This displays the Projector settings window where you can choose how to display your desktop.

 For more about the specifics of using your cellphone with a wireless network connection, check your phone manufacturer's user manual.

Turn On Presentation Settings

1. By turning on presentation settings, you disable your screen saver, which avoids having your screen go black or displaying a screen saver in the middle of a presentation. Choose Start➪Control Panel and click the Adjust Common Mobility Settings under the Sound and Hardware topic.

2. In the Windows Mobility Center window that appears, as shown in Figure 9-10, click the Turn On button for Presentation Settings.

3. When you're done with your presentation, repeat this procedure and click the Turn Off button in Step 2.

 If you use a Tablet PC, a setting in the Windows Mobility Center can change the orientation of your screen from landscape to portrait. If you're connected to a projector for a presentation, that display shifts as well.

Figure 9-10: The Windows Mobility Center

Part III

Setting Up Hardware and Networks

The 5th Wave — By Rich Tennant

"That's it! We're getting a wireless network for the house."

Setting Up New Hardware

Peripherals, graphics cards, modems, USB sticks — just what the heck is all this stuff?

Collectively, these items belong to the *computer hardware* category. Your CPU and monitor are hardware. So are the cards slotted into your CPU that provide memory to run software and the mechanisms for playing sounds and videos. Printers are hardware, as is anything else that plugs into your computer.

Installing a new piece of hardware used to be a great occasion for groaning and moaning. Nothing was compatible, everything installed differently, and Windows itself didn't have much in the way of popular *drivers* (software that runs various pieces of hardware) ready and waiting. That all changed with *Plug and Play* technology, which automates the installation process and some standardizing of connections through Universal Serial Bus (USB) ports. Windows now comes with a full framework of drivers for hardware devices, and whatever it doesn't have is usually easy to download from any hardware manufacturer's Web site. In this chapter, you find out how you can

➡ **Install and set up common peripherals.** Peripherals include a monitor, printer, and modem.

➡ **Install and set up cards that slot into your CPU.** Add sound and video cards.

➡ **Partition your hard drive.** Add hard drive partitions to optimize memory.

Get ready to . . .

Install a Printer

1. Read the instructions that came with the printer. Some printers require that you install software before connecting them, but others can be connected right away.

2. Turn on your computer and then follow the option that fits your needs:

   - If your printer is a Plug and Play device, connect it; Windows installs what it needs automatically.

   - Insert the disc that came with the device and follow the onscreen instructions.

   - Choose Start➪Devices and Printers. If this is the option that you're following, proceed to the next step in this list.

3. If you choose the third option in Step 2, in the Devices and Printers window that appears, click the Add a Printer link near the top.

4. In the resulting wizard window (the Add Printer dialog box, as shown in Figure 10-1), click the Add a Local Printer option and click Next.

5. In the Choose a Printer Port dialog box shown in Figure 10-2, click the down arrow on the Use an Existing Port field and select a port, or just use the recommended port setting that Windows selects for you. Click Next.

Figure 10-1: The Add Printer Wizard

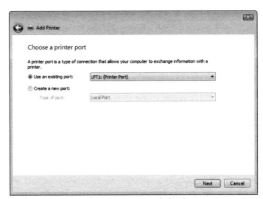

Figure 10-2: The Select a Printer Port dialog box

6. In the next wizard window (Install the Printer Driver dialog box; see Figure 10-3), choose a manufacturer and then choose a printer. You then have two options:

   • If you have the manufacturer's disc, insert it in the appropriate CD drive now and click the Have Disk button. Click Next.

   • If you don't have the manufacturer's disc, click the Windows Update button to see a list of printer drivers that you can download from the Microsoft Web site. Click Next.

7. In the resulting Type a Printer Name dialog box (see Figure 10-4), enter a printer name and click Next.

8. In the resulting dialog box, click Finish to complete the Add Printer Wizard.

 If your computer is on a network, you get an additional dialog box in the wizard right after you name the printer. Select the Do Not Share This Printer option to stop others from using the printer, or you can select the Share Name option and enter a printer name to share the printer on your network. This means that others can see and select this printer to print to.

Figure 10-3: The Install Printer Driver dialog box

Figure 10-4: The Type a Printer Name dialog box

Set a Default Printer

1. Choose Start⇨Devices and Printers.

2. In the resulting Devices and Printers window (as shown in Figure 10-5), the current default printer is indicated by a check mark.

3. Right-click any printer that isn't set as the default and choose Set as Default Printer from the shortcut menu, as shown in Figure 10-6.

4. Click the Close button in the Devices and Printers window to save the new settings.

 To modify printing properties (for example, whether the printer prints in draft or high-quality mode, or whether it uses color or only black and white), right-click a printer in the Devices and Printers window (see Figure 10-6) and choose Printing Preferences. This same dialog box is available from most common Windows-based software programs, such as Microsoft Word or Excel, by clicking the Properties button in the Print dialog box.

 If you right-click the printer that's already set as the default, you'll find that the Set as Default Printer command isn't available on the shortcut menu mentioned in Step 3.

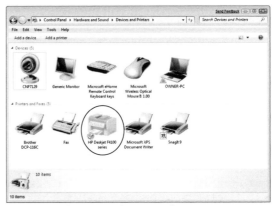

Figure 10-5: The Devices and Printers window

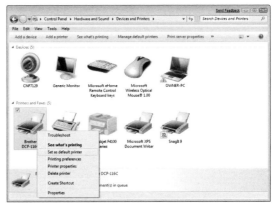

Figure 10-6: The shortcut menu to set a default printer

Configure a USB Device

1. Choose Start➪Control Panel➪Hardware and Sound➪ Device Manager.

2. In the resulting Device Manager dialog box (see Figure 10-7), click the plus sign to the left of the Universal Serial Bus Controllers item. Right-click an item and choose Properties.

3. In the resulting Properties dialog box, click the Driver tab, as shown in Figure 10-8. Here you can disable or enable the device by clicking the Disable/Enable button (the name depends on whether the device is currently enabled or disabled).

4. Click any of the other buttons to view details about the driver, update it to a newer version, or uninstall it.

5. Click OK to save your USB device settings.

 If a USB device isn't working properly, click the Resources tab of the USB Device Properties dialog box. This includes a list of any conflicting devices that could be causing problems. Also, check the Help and Support Center for Windows (Start➪Help and Support) to locate troubleshooting help.

Figure 10-7: The Device Manager dialog box

Figure 10-8: The Driver tab

Set Up a New Monitor

1. Place the CD that came with your monitor in your CD-ROM drive and choose Start⇨Control Panel⇨ Hardware and Sound⇨Device Manager.

2. In the resulting Device Manager window, click the plus sign to the left of Monitors to display installed monitors (see Figure 10-9). Right-click the new monitor and choose Scan for Hardware Changes from the shortcut menu.

3. If your monitor driver is up to date, you see a message that scanning is in progress, which disappears when the scan is complete. If your monitor driver isn't up to date, the Hardware Update Wizard appears. Follow the wizard screens to install the monitor drivers.

4. When the wizard is complete, if everything seems to be working fine, you can close the Device Manager window.

 If you have problems with the monitor, open the Device Manager window, right-click the monitor, and then choose Properties. In the Driver tab of the resulting Monitor Properties dialog box, make sure that the fourth button says Disable (which means the monitor is enabled). If things still aren't working right, check out Windows Help and Support for troubleshooting advice.

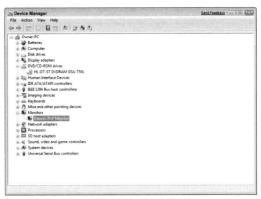

Figure 10-9: Monitors displayed in the Device Manager

 Many manufacturers' device drivers are already stored in Windows. When you install a device by using the Hardware Update Wizard, you might find that you can simply browse the manufacturers' device drivers rather than download them or select them from a CD.

 You can make adjustments to your monitor display by using the Appearance and Personalization category of the Control Panel. For more about making Display option settings, take a gander at Chapter 12.

Upgrade a Graphics Card

1. Turn off your computer. (*Note:* This step is very important; you have to open your CPU for this procedure, and you're in danger of severe electrical shock if you leave your computer on while you play around inside it. Also, don't perform this task on a laptop computer.)

2. Refer to your computer manual to determine how to open the CPU, how your computer is configured, where graphics cards can be inserted, and which kinds of graphics cards to use.

3. Plug the graphics card into the appropriate slot, close your computer, and replace any screws that you took out when opening the computer.

4. Turn on the computer; Windows detects the new card and installs appropriate drivers.

5. View the information about the installed graphics device by choosing Start⇨Control Panel⇨Hardware and Sound⇨Device Manager.

6. Click the plus sign next to Display Adapters (see Figure 10-10), right-click the graphics card that you installed, and then choose Properties. You see system settings for this card (see Figure 10-11). The Device Status tells you whether it's working properly.

 Note that your particular hardware might have its own idiosyncrasies, and new technologies come along that change the way newer computers are configured, so be sure to read your computer user's manual before dealing with any hardware upgrade.

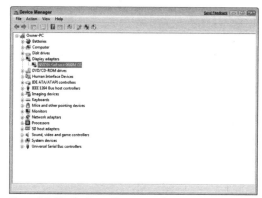

Figure 10-10: The Device Manager window

Figure 10-11: Assessing the status of your new graphics card

 Warning: Be careful about poking metal implements (such as screwdrivers) into the insides of the CPU because you could set off an electrical unpleasantry. Place your computer on a nonconductive surface (such as a rubber mat) before opening it up. Don't wear an aluminum foil suit for this sort of procedure, and ***never*** leave your computer plugged in or turned on while opening it.

Set Up a Sound Card

1. Choose Start⇨Control Panel⇨Hardware and Sound, and then click the Device Manager link.

2. In the resulting Device Manager window (see Figure 10-12), click the plus sign icon to the left of Sound, Video, and Game Controllers.

3. Right-click the sound card listed there and choose Properties.

4. In the resulting Audio Device Properties dialog box, click the Driver tab, shown in Figure 10-13, and if the fourth button down is labeled Enable, click it to enable the device.

5. If you want to make changes to the driver, click the Update Driver button.

6. When you're done making settings, click OK.

 Read your user's manual before doing this procedure. Some sound cards are built into the motherboard, but others require that you take some steps to disable the old card before installing the new.

 If you're having trouble getting sound, remember the basics: You have to have speakers connected to your computer and turn the speaker power on, and the volume setting on your computer can't be muted. If you neglect to properly set these vital requirements, don't be ashamed — just about everyone has done it, myself included!

Figure 10-12: The Device Manager window

Figure 10-13: The Audio Device Properties dialog box, Driver tab

Use Disk Management to Extend a Partition

1. Choose Start⇨Control Panel⇨System and Security⇨ Administrative Tools.

2. In the resulting Administrative Tools windows, double-click Computer Management.

3. In the resulting Computer Management window (as shown in Figure 10-14), click Disk Management in the list on the left, right-click a basic disk in the top center pane (this is usually your hard drive) that isn't allocated, and then choose Extend Volume from the shortcut menu that appears (see Figure 10-15).

4. Follow the steps in the New Simple Volume Wizard to create the new partition.

> An extended partition adds to your drive space by borrowing some from an adjoining partition and makes your system utilize memory more efficiently. But just so you know, you have to be logged on as a system administrator to complete the steps listed here.

> You can also shrink a drive, which frees up some space for you to create a new partition at the end of a volume. The Shrink Volume command is located on the shortcut menu that appears when you right-click a disk in the Disk Management window.

Figure 10-14: The Computer Management window

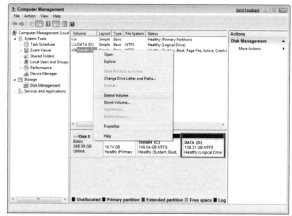

Figure 10-15: The Disk Management window

Setting Up a Network

Setting up a network among two or more computers can make your life much easier because after you set up a network, you can use this connection to share files, folders, printers, and access to the Internet with other users.

The most common way to connect a network is to use a wired Ethernet connection, involving cables and equipment, referred to as a *hub* or *switch*. To determine whether your computer is Ethernet-ready, check the back of your PC or the side of your laptop: You should see what looks like a very large phone connector jack. This is the Ethernet connector.

After you connect the necessary cables and equipment, most newer computers already have network drivers installed, so Windows 7 is capable of recognizing the connection. With simple-to-use wizards, little input on your part is required to set up a network.

You can also set up a connection through a wireless access point (which you set up according to the instructions that come with the wireless router) and an adapter that you either install in your CPU in the form of a *PCI* (*Peripheral Component Interconnect,* used for attaching hardware devices to your computer) adapter or plug into your PC by using a USB (Universal Serial Bus) port or a PC Card adapter.

To set up a network, you explore the following tasks:

➡ Installing a network adapter if one isn't built into your computer and configuring a network by using the Network Setup Wizard

➡ Setting up a wireless access point and configuring a wireless network by using the Wireless Network Setup Wizard

➡ Making various settings to a network connection, including changing a networked computer's name so the one you gave it when you bought it isn't the one that shows on the network

➡ Creating and viewing workgroups on a network

➡ Creating a Bluetooth connection

Chapter 11

Get ready to . . .

Install a PCI Network Adapter

1. After purchasing the PCI adapter, turn off your desktop computer and disconnect all power and other cables from it.

2. Open the PC chassis (see Figure 11-1). Check your user's manual for this procedure, which usually involves removing a few screws and popping the cover off your tower.

3. Touch a metal object (not the computer) to get rid of any static discharge before you reach inside the computer.

4. Locate an empty slot for the PCI adapter and, if necessary, remove the protective cover from it. Again, check your manual for the exact location in your system.

5. Remove the adapter from its packaging. Handling it by its edges, line it up with the slot and insert it firmly but gently.

6. Make sure you don't disconnect any wires or leave loose screws inside the PC chassis; then replace the computer cover and reinsert the screws.

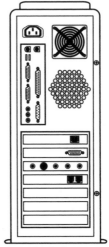

Figure 11-1: Opening your CPU case

 Leave the parts that you're going to insert in your computer in their packaging until you need them. If they sit around on your desktop or elsewhere, they could pick up static discharge, which could be harmful to your computer.

7. Plug in the computer and turn it on. Your computer senses the new adapter when it starts up and displays the Installing Device Driver Software pop-up above your taskbar (see Figure 11-2).

8. Windows might automatically set up the hardware. If Windows can't find a driver for the adapter, you might have to provide it.

9. When the process is complete, a pop-up appears stating that your hardware driver is installed and ready to use (see Figure 11-3).

 If Windows can't find the driver, use the DVD or CD that came with the adapter — or you can usually download the driver from your hardware manufacturer's Web site for free. Use the Browse button to navigate to the location where you downloaded the driver and then proceed with the wizard.

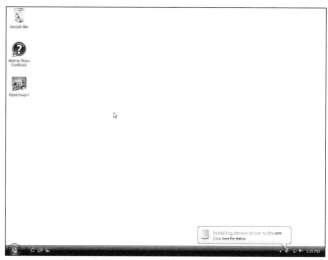

Figure 11-2: The Installing Device Driver Software pop-up

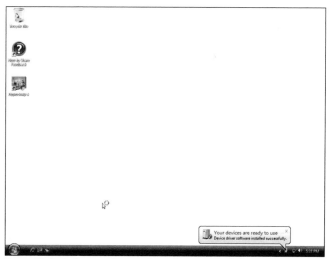

Figure 11-3: Confirmation that your device driver was installed

Connect a Wired Ethernet Network

1. Obtain a Cat 5 or Cat 5e Ethernet cable for every computer you'll connect to the network (see Figure 11-4).

2. Purchase a hub or switch with enough ports for each computer you want to connect (see Figure 11-5) and maybe a few extras for future expansion.

3. Turn off all computers as well as the switch/hub. Plug one end of the Ethernet cable into the switch or hub and the other end into the network adapter that you installed in your PC. See the first task in this chapter for help with this.

4. Repeat Step 3 for each computer you want to include in the network.

5. Turn on the switch or hub and then turn on the computers. Use the following task to run the Network Setup Wizard and set up the network.

 Switches make for a speedier network, although they cost a little more than a hub. However, in most cases, it's better to invest a few dollars more for the extra performance of a switch. If you want to get very sophisticated — for example, like on a company network — you could use a router, which helps you track various people on the network and the places they're going on the network.

 Cat 5 is a kind of cable used for data transfer. If your home is wired for high speed access, you may have Cat 5 cable in your walls. You can find the kind of Cat 5 cable referred to in this task at your local computer or office supply store with connectors for plugging into your computer and hub.

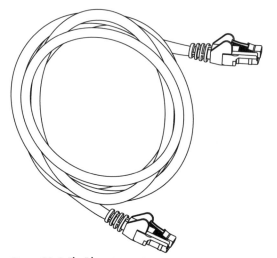

Figure 11-4: The Ethernet connector

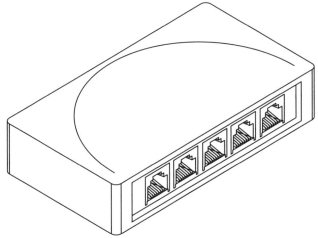

Figure 11-5: A switch with ports

Configure a Wireless Network by Using the Network Setup Wizard

1. Turn on each PC that you have attached to the network.

2. On the PC that will share its Internet connection, log on to the Internet.

3. On the Internet-connection PC, choose Start⇨Control Panel⇨Network and Internet and then click the Network and Sharing Center link.

4. In the resulting Network and Sharing Center window (see Figure 11-6), click the Set Up a New Connection or Network link.

5. In the resulting Choose a Connection Option window, choose the Set Up a Wireless Ad Hoc (Computer-to-Computer) Network option and then click Next. The next window describes what the wizard will do; click Next.

(This task is continued on the next page.)

When you purchase a wireless access point, it includes instructions for setting it up. This typically involves plugging it into a power source, plugging in Ethernet cables to your main computer and possibly a DSL (digital subscriber line) or other high speed modem, and then turning it on.

Figure 11-6: The Network and Sharing window

6. In the following window (see Figure 11-7), enter a Network Name, choose a Security Type, and enter a Security Key/Passphrase. If you need help choosing security options, click the Help Me Choose link. Click Next.

7. A progress windows displays while Windows detects your hardware settings. You have a few options at this point:

   • Windows detects your hardware and configures it automatically; you're done.

   • Windows detects your hardware but requires you to configure it manually. In this case, select the Configure This Device Manually option and complete the required information to finish the setup.

   • If you have a Flash drive connected via a USB port, connect the drive and click Create Wireless Network Settings and Save to a USB Flash Drive. Enter a name for your network on the following screen and then follow the directions, which involve disconnecting the Flash drive and plugging it into a wireless access point. You can then use the drive to configure each computer on the network as directed.

8. On the final wizard screen that appears, click Finish.

Figure 11-7: Choosing how to set up your network

 If your wireless connection seems slow, there could be several reasons for that. One factor to consider is whether you've protected your computer from spyware and viruses. If these are downloaded to your computer hard drive, they can gradually slow down its performance. In addition, the amount of memory in each computer and the condition of the hard drives can play a role, so you may find two computers sharing the same network actually access the Internet through your network at different speeds. If you have a lot of programs running, that can slow down your connection speed as well.

Change a Computer's Network Name

1. Two computers on the same network can't have the same name. Therefore, you may want to modify computer names before you start setting up your network so they're unique. Choose Start⇨Control Panel⇨ System and Security and then click the System link.

2. In the resulting System window, as shown in Figure 11-8, click the Change Settings link.

3. On the Computer Name tab of the resulting System Properties dialog box, as shown in Figure 11-9, replace the current name with a name in the Computer Description text box and then click OK to save the new name.

4. Click the Close button to close the Control Panel.

 Making the computer name descriptive is useful: Simple names, such as *John's Computer* and *Basement PC,* help everybody on the network know which is which.

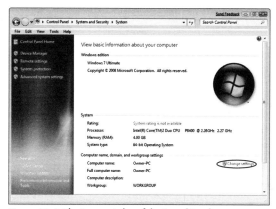

Figure 11-8: The System window of the Control Panel

Figure 11-9: The System Properties dialog box, Computer Name tab

Join a Workgroup

1. Choose Start⇨Control Panel⇨System and Security and then click the System link.

2. In the resulting System window, as shown in Figure 11-10, click the Change Settings link.

3. On the Computer Name tab of the resulting System Properties dialog box, click the Change button.

4. The Computer Name/Domain Changes dialog box appears (see Figure 11-11). In the Workgroup field, enter or edit the name for your workgroup *with no spaces between letters.*

5. Click OK to close the dialog box and then click OK again to close the System Properties dialog box. If prompted, restart Windows 7.

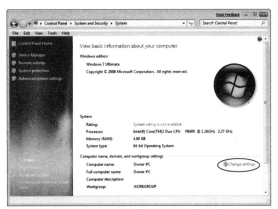

Figure 11-10: The System window

A *workgroup* is essentially a set of computers on a network. On a large network, breaking down computers into these groups so they can easily work with each other makes sense. In a smaller home network, you'll probably just create one workgroup to allow all your computers to easily access each other.

One task that becomes easier when you're part of a workgroup is sharing files. If you locate a file or a folder on your computer and right-click it, you can choose to share it on the network. When you do, only people in your workgroup can access this shared file or folder.

Figure 11-11: The Computer Name/ Domain Changes dialog box

Choose Sharing Options

1. Your network connects computers on a home network to share files and printers, but you may want to adjust your sharing settings. Choose Start➪Control Panel➪ Network and Internet.

2. In the resulting window, click the Homegroup link. In the Homegroup window, click the Change Advanced Sharing Settings link.

3. In the resulting window, as shown in Figure 11-12, use the radio buttons to make settings for sharing on both Home or Work networks and Public networks. For example, if you want to share files and printers, turn on that setting; if you want to share your public folder contents, turn that on; and so on.

4. Click the Save Changes button to save the settings.

 You have to connect to a network to use your sharing options. Click the Network icon on the system tray, click a connection, and then click Connect to do so.

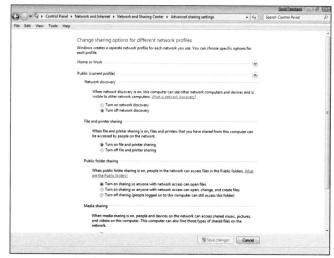

Figure 11-12: The Advanced Sharing Settings dialog box

Part IV
Customizing Windows

The 5th Wave   By Rich Tennant

"The funny thing is he's spent 9 hours organizing his computer desktop."

Setting Up Your Display

*Y*ou chose your designer Day Planner, glow-in-the-dark gel pens, and solid maple inbox for your real-world desktop, right? Why shouldn't the Windows desktop give you the same flexibility to make things look the way you like? After all, this is the main work area of Windows, a space that you traverse many, many times in a typical workday. Take it from somebody who spends many hours in front of a computer: Customizing your desktop pays off in increased productivity as well as decreased eyestrain.

To customize your desktop, you can do the following:

➡ Set up Windows to display images and colors.

➡ Use screen saver settings to switch from everyday work stuff to a pretty animation when you've stopped working for a time.

➡ You can modify your *screen resolution* setting, which controls how sharp and detailed a picture your screen displays.

➡ Make text larger or smaller. You can change the size of all text on your screen with an easy setting. (See Chapter 13 for more about settings that help those with visual challenges.)

Chapter 12

Get ready to . . .

Set Your Screen's Resolution

1. Choose Start⇨Control Panel⇨Appearance and Personalization and click the Adjust Screen Resolution link.

2. In the resulting Screen Resolution window, click the arrow to the right of the Resolution field.

3. Use the slider (as shown in Figure 12-1) to select a higher or lower resolution. You can also change the orientation of your display by making a choice in the Orientation drop-down list.

4. Click OK to accept the new screen resolution.

 Higher resolutions, such as 1400 x 1250, produce smaller, crisper images. Lower resolutions, such as 800 x 600, produce larger, somewhat jagged images. The upside of higher resolution is that more fits on your screen; the downside is that words and graphics can be hard to see.

 The Advanced Settings link in the Screen Resolution dialog box displays another dialog box where you can work with color management and monitor settings.

 Remember that you can also use your View settings in most software programs to get a larger or smaller view of your documents without having to change your screen's resolution.

Figure 12-1: The Screen Resolution dialog box

Change the Desktop Background

1. Right-click the desktop and choose Personalize from the shortcut menu.

2. In the resulting Personalization window, click the Desktop Background link to display the Desktop Background dialog box, as shown in Figure 12-2.

3. Select a category of desktop background options from the Picture Location list box (see Figure 12-3) and then click the image preview you want to use. The background is previewed on your desktop.

4. Click Save Changes to apply the settings and close the dialog box.

 If you apply a desktop theme (see the next task), you overwrite whatever desktop settings you've made in this task. If you apply a desktop theme and then go back and make desktop settings, you replace the theme's settings. However, making changes is easy and keeps your desktop interesting, so play around with themes and desktop backgrounds all you like! If you make settings you like, you can save those settings as a custom theme so you can apply them again at any time by clicking the Save As button in the Theme Settings dialog box.

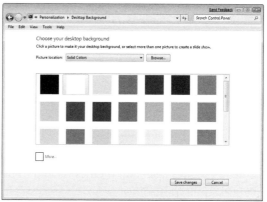

Figure 12-2: The Desktop Background dialog box

Figure 12-3: Available categories of backgrounds

Choose a Desktop Theme

1. Right-click the desktop and choose Personalize. The Personalization window opens.

2. In the resulting Personalization dialog box, as shown in Figure 12-4, select a theme. Your options include the following:

   - **My Themes** uses whatever settings you have and saves them with that name.

   - **Windows Themes** offers up themes related to nature, landscapes, and light auras, and your country of residence.

   - **Ease of Access Themes** offer a variety of easy to read contrast settings in a variety of themes.

3. Click Close to close the dialog box.

 Themes save sets of elements that include menu appearance, background colors or patterns, screen savers, and even mouse cursors and sounds. If you modify any of these individually — for example, by changing the screen saver to another one — that change overrides the setting in the theme you last applied.

 You can save custom themes. Simply apply a theme, make any changes to it you like with the various Appearance and Personalization settings options, and then in the Personalization dialog box, click Save Theme. In the resulting dialog box, give your new theme a name and click Save. It now appears in the Theme list.

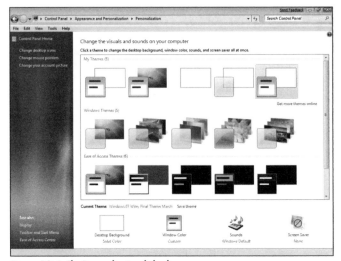

Figure 12-4: The Personalization dialog box

Set Up a Screen Saver

1. Right-click the desktop and choose Personalize. In the resulting Personalization window, click the Screen Saver button to display the Screen Saver Settings dialog box, as shown in Figure 12-5.

2. From the Screen Saver drop-down list, choose a screen saver.

3. Use the arrows in the Wait *xx* Minutes text box to set the number of inactivity minutes that Windows 7 waits before displaying the screen saver.

4. Click the Preview button to take a peek at your screen saver of choice (see Figure 12-6). When you're happy with your settings, click OK.

Figure 12-5: The Screen Saver Settings dialog box

 Screen savers used to be required to keep your monitor from burning out because an image was held on your screen for too long. Newer monitors don't require this, but people are attached to their screen savers, so the feature persists. Screen savers are also useful for hiding what's on your screen from curious passersby if you happen to wander away from your desk for a while. If you don't want a screen saver to appear, choose None from the Screen Saver list in the Screen Saver Settings dialog box.

 Some screen savers allow you to modify their settings: for example, how fast they display or how many lines they draw onscreen. To customize this, click the Settings button in the Screen Saver Settings dialog box.

Figure 12-6: The Ribbons screen saver preview

Change the Windows 7 Color Scheme

1. Right-click the desktop and choose Personalize.

2. In the resulting Personalization window, click the Window Color button to display the Window Color and Appearance dialog box, as shown in Figure 12-7.

3. Select items one by one from the Item drop-down list. Make any changes you wish by using the Size, Color, and Font settings.

4. Click OK to accept the settings and then click the Close button to close the Personalization dialog box.

 When customizing a color scheme, be aware that not all screen elements allow you to modify all settings. For example, setting an Application Background doesn't make the Font setting available — because it's just a background setting. Makes sense, huh?

 Some colors are easier on the eyes than others. For example, green is more restful to look at than orange. Choose a color scheme that's pleasant to look at and easy on the eyes!

Figure 12-7: The Window Color and Appearance dialog box

Make Text Larger or Smaller

1. Choose Start⇨Control Panel⇨Appearance and Personalization. Click Make Text and Other Items Larger or Smaller in the resulting window.

2. In the resulting Display window (see Figure 12-8), click the radio button for the text size you prefer. Smaller is the default, but you can expand the text size to 125 percent with the Medium setting and 150 percent with the Larger setting.

3. Click the Close button to close the dialog box and see the results (see Figure 12-9, which shows the Larger setting applied).

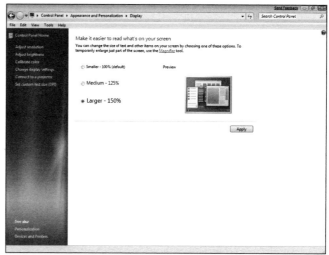

Figure 12-8: The Display dialog box

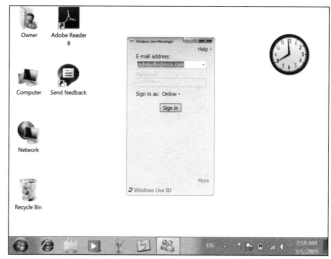

Figure 12-9: The Larger text setting applied

Customize Windows Ease of Access

*P*eople aren't born with good manners. Everyone has to be taught to help other people and share toys, for example. Similarly, sometimes Windows has to be taught how to behave. For example, Windows doesn't know right off the bat that somebody using it has a vision challenge that requires special help, or that a user prefers a certain mouse cursor, or has difficulty using a keyboard.

Somebody taught you manners, but Windows depends on you to make settings that customize its behavior. This is good news for you because the ability to customize Windows gives you a lot of flexibility in how you interact with it.

Here's what you can do to customize Windows:

➡ Control features that help visually challenged users to work with a computer, such as setting a higher contrast or using a Narrator to read the onscreen text aloud.

➡ Work with the Speech Recognition feature that allows you to input data into a document using speech rather than a keyboard or a mouse.

➡ Modify the mouse functionality for left-handed use, change the cursor to sport a certain look, or make viewing the cursor as it moves around your screen easier.

➡ Work with keyboard settings that make input easier for those who are challenged by physical conditions, such as carpal tunnel syndrome or arthritis.

Chapter 13

Get ready to . . .

Optimize the Visual Display

1. Choose Start⇨Control Panel.

2. In the Control Panel window, click the Optimize Visual Display link under the Ease of Access tools.

3. In the resulting Make the Computer Easier to See dialog box (as shown in Figure 13-1), select the check boxes for features you want to use:

- **High Contrast**: By choosing this setting you can turn on higher contrast with a keystroke shortcut (Alt+Shift+Print Screen). High Contrast is a color scheme that makes your screen easier to read.

- **Hear Text and Descriptions Read Aloud:** You can turn on a Narrator feature that will read onscreen text or an Audio Description feature to describe what's happening in video programs.

- **Make Things on the Screen Larger:** If you click Turn on Magnifier, you have two cursors onscreen. One cursor appears in the Magnifier window where everything is shown enlarged, and one appears in whatever is showing on your computer (for example, your desktop or an open application). You can maneuver either cursor to work in your document.

- **Make Things On the Screen Easier to See:** Here's where you make settings that adjust onscreen contrast to make things easier to see, enlarge the size of the blinking mouse cursor (see Figure 13-2), and get rid of distracting animations and backgrounds.

4. When you finish making settings, click Apply to apply them and keep the window open, or OK to apply the settings and close the window.

Figure 13-1: The Make the Computer Easier to See dialog box

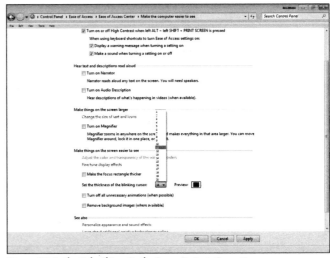

Figure 13-2: The Make Things On the Screen Easier to See settings

Replace Sounds with Visual Cues

1. Choose Start⇨Control Panel⇨Ease of Access and then click the Replace Sounds with Visual Cues link.

2. In the resulting Use Text or Visual Alternatives for Sounds dialog box (see Figure 13-3), make any of the following settings:

   • You can select Turn On Visual Notifications for Sound (Sound Sentry) so that Windows will play sounds along with a display of visual cues.

   • Choose a setting for visual warnings. These warnings essentially flash a portion of your screen to alert you to an event.

   • To control text captions for any spoken words, select Turn On Text Captions for Spoken Dialog. *Note:* This isn't always available with every application you use.

3. To save the new settings, click OK.

 Visual cues are useful if you're hard of hearing and don't always pick up system sounds alerting you to error messages or a device disconnect. After the setting is turned on, it's active until you go back to the Use Text or Visual Alternatives for Sounds dialog box and turn it off.

Figure 13-3: The Use Text or Visual Alternatives for Sounds dialog box

 This may seem obvious, but if you're hard of hearing, you may want to simply increase the volume for your speakers. You can do this by using the volume adjustment in a program, such as Windows Media Player (see Chapter 21), or modifying your system volume by choosing Hardware and Sound in the Control Panel and then clicking the Adjust System Volume link.

Set Up Speech Recognition

1. Attach a desktop microphone or headset to your computer and choose Start⇨Control Panel⇨Ease of Access⇨Start Speech Recognition.

2. The Welcome to Speech Recognition message appears; click Next to continue. (*Note:* If you've used Speech Recognition before, this message won't appear.)

3. In the resulting Microphone Setup Wizard (as shown in Figure 13-4), select the type of microphone that you're using and then click Next. The next screen tells you how to place and use the microphone for optimum results. Click Next.

4. In the following window (see Figure 13-5), read the sample sentence aloud. When you're done, click Next. A window appears telling you that your microphone is now set up. Click Next.

 During the Speech Recognition setup procedure, you're given the option of printing commonly used commands. It's a good idea to do this, as speech commands aren't always second nature!

5. In the resulting dialog box, choose whether to enable or disable document view. Document view allows Windows to review your documents and e-mail to help it recognize your speech patterns. Click Next.

Figure 13-4: The Microphone Setup Wizard

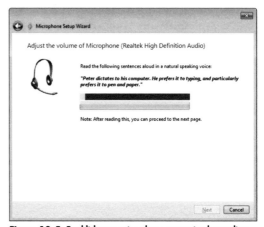

Figure 13-5: Establish your microphone connection by reading a sentence aloud

6. In the resulting dialog box, choose either manual activation mode where you can use a mouse, pen, or keyboard to turn the feature on; or voice activation, which is useful if you have difficulty manipulating devices because of arthritis or hand injury. Click Next.

7. In the resulting screen, if you wish to view and/or print a list of speech recognition commands, click the View Reference Sheet button and read about or print reference information, and then click the Close button to close that window. Click Next to proceed.

8. In the resulting dialog box, either click Run Speech Recognition at Startup to disable this feature or leave the default setting. Click Next. The final dialog box informs you that you can now control the computer by voice and offers you a Start Tutorial button to help you practice voice commands. Click that button, or click Skip Tutorial to skip the tutorial and leave the Speech Recognition setup.

9. The Speech Recognition Control Panel appears (see Figure 13-6). Say "Start listening" to activate the feature if you used voice activation in Step 6, or click the Start Speech Recognition link if you chose manual activation in Step 6. You can now begin using spoken commands to work with your computer.

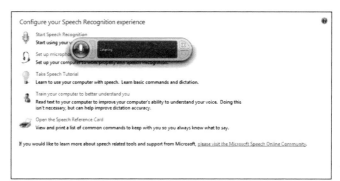

Configure your Speech Recognition experience

Start Speech Recognition
Start using your...

Set up microphone
Set up your computer to work properly with speech recognition.

Take Speech Tutorial
Learn to use your computer with speech. Learn basic commands and dictation.

Train your computer to better understand you
Read text to your computer to improve your computer's ability to understand your voice. Doing this isn't necessary, but can help improve dictation accuracy.

Open the Speech Reference Card
View and print a list of common commands to keep with you so you always know what to say.

If you would like to learn more about speech related tools and support from Microsoft, please visit the Microsoft Speech Online Community.

Figure 13-6: The Speech Recognition Control Panel

To stop Speech Recognition, click the Close button on the Control Panel. To start the Speech Recognition feature again, choose Start⇨ Control Panel⇨Ease of Access⇨Speech Recognition and then click the Start Speech Recognition link. To read more about Speech Recognition commands, click the Take Speech Tutorials link in the Speech Recognition Options window accessed from the Ease of Access window of the Control Panel.

Modify How Your Keyboard Works

1. Choose Start➪Control Panel➪Ease of Access and then click the Change How Your Keyboard Works link.

2. In the resulting Make the Keyboard Easier to Use dialog box (see Figure 13-7), make any of these settings:

   • Turn On Mouse Keys to control your mouse by keyboard commands. If you turn on this setting, click the Set Up Mouse Keys link to specify settings for this feature.

   • Select the Turn On Sticky Keys feature to enable keystroke combinations to be pressed one at a time, rather than in combination.

   • Turn On Toggle Keys. You can set up Windows to play a sound when you press Caps Lock, Num Lock, or Scroll Lock (which I do all the time by mistake!).

   • If you sometimes press a key very lightly or press it so hard it activates twice, you can use the Turn On Filter Keys setting to adjust repeat rates. Use the Set Up Filter Keys link to fine-tune settings if you make this choice.

   • To have Windows highlight keyboard shortcuts and access keys with an underline wherever these shortcuts appear, click that setting.

   • If you want to avoid having windows shift automatically when you move them to the edge of your screen, use the Make It Easier to Manage Windows setting.

3. To save the new settings, click OK.

Figure 13-7: The Make the Keyboard Easier to Use dialog box

 You can click the Learn about Additional Assistive Technologies Online link to go to the Microsoft Web site and discover add-on and third party programs that might help you if you have a visual, hearing, or input-related disability.

 Keyboards all have their own unique feel. If your keyboard isn't responsive and you have a keyboard-challenging condition, you might also try different keyboards to see whether one works better for you than another.

Use the On-Screen Keyboard Feature

1. Choose Start⇨Control Panel⇨Ease of Access.

2. In the resulting Ease of Access Center dialog box (see Figure 13-8), click Start On-Screen Keyboard. The On-Screen Keyboard appears (see Figure 13-9).

3. Open a document in any application where you can enter text, and then click the keys on the On-Screen Keyboard to make entries.

 To use keystroke combinations (such as Ctrl+Z), click the first key (in this case, Ctrl) and then click the second key (Z). You don't have to hold down the first key as you do with a regular keyboard.

4. To change settings, such as how you select keys (Typing Mode) or the font used to label keys (Font), click the Options key on the On-Screen Keyboard, choose one of the four options shown in the Options dialog box, and click OK.

5. Click the Close button on the On-Screen Keyboard to stop using it.

 You can set up the Hover typing mode to activate a key after you hover your mouse over it for a predefined period of time (x number of seconds). If you have arthritis or some other condition that makes clicking your mouse difficult, this option can help you enter text. Click the Hover Over Keys item in the Options dialog box and use the slider to set how long you have to hover before activating the key.

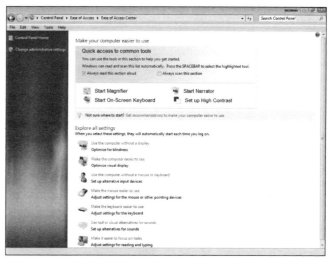

Figure 13-8: The Ease of Access Center

Figure 13-9: The On-Screen Keyboard

Change Mouse Behavior

1. Choose Start⇨Control Panel⇨Ease of Access and then click the Change How Your Mouse Works link. The Make the Mouse Easier to Use dialog box opens (see Figure 13-10).

2. To use the numeric keypad to move your mouse cursor on your screen, choose the Turn On Mouse Keys setting. If you turn on this feature, click Set Up Mouse Keys to fine-tune its behavior.

3. Select the Activate a Window by Hovering Over It with the Mouse check box to enable this (pretty self-explanatory!) feature.

4. Click OK to save the new settings.

 If you're left-handed, click the Mouse Settings link in the Make the Mouse Easier to Use dialog box; then, on the Buttons tab, use the Switch Primary and Secondary Buttons feature to make the right mouse button handle all the usual left button functions, such as clicking and dragging, and the left button handle the typical right-hand functions, such as displaying shortcut menus. This helps left-handed people use the mouse more easily.

 If you want to modify the behavior of the mouse pointer, in the Mouse Properties dialog box, click the Pointer Options tab to set the *pointer speed* (how quickly you can drag the mouse pointer around your screen), to activate the Snap To feature that automatically moves the mouse cursor to the default choice in a dialog box, or to modify the little trails that appear when you drag the pointer.

Figure 13-10: The Make the Mouse Easier to Use dialog box

 If you have difficulty seeing the cursor onscreen, experiment with the Windows 7 color schemes to see if another setting makes your cursor stand out better against the background. See Chapter 12 for information on setting up the color scheme for your computer.

Change the Cursor

1. Choose Start➪Control Panel➪Ease of Access➪Change How Your Mouse Works. In the resulting Make the Mouse Easier to Use dialog box, click the Mouse Settings link.

2. In the resulting Mouse Properties dialog box, on the Pointers tab, as shown in Figure 13-11, click to select a pointer, such as Normal Select, and then click the Browse button. In the Browse dialog box that appears, click an alternate cursor and then click Open.

3. Click Apply to use the new pointer setting and then click OK to close the Mouse Properties dialog box.

 Be careful not to change the cursor to another standard cursor (for example, changing the Normal Select cursor to the Busy hourglass cursor). This could prove slightly confusing for you and completely baffling to anybody else who works on your computer. If you make a choice and decide it was a mistake, click the Use Default button on the Pointers tab in the Mouse Properties dialog box to return a selected cursor to its default choice.

 You can also choose the color and size of mouse pointers in the Make the Mouse Easier to Use dialog box. A large white or extra large black cursor might be more visible to you, depending on the color scheme you have applied to Windows 7.

Figure 13-11: The Mouse Properties dialog box

Part V
Using Security and Maintenance Features

The 5th Wave   By Rich Tennant

"Well, the first level of Windows 7 security seems good—I can't get the shrink-wrapping off."

Setting Passwords and File Access

Chapter 14

After working with Windows and the software that it supports for a while, you'll find that you've amassed a treasure trove of information and documents. Microsoft provides features in Windows that help to keep your computer private, whether at work or home, as well as to protect your valuable files. These features include the following:

➡ With passwords assigned (password-protection), you can keep people from accessing your computer when you're not around.

➡ Shared and public folder features allow you to share information with others on a network or to keep others out of folders, if you prefer. You can also use the shared folders feature to share folders with multiple users of a standalone computer.

➡ Use settings to protect individual files by making them *read-only* — that is, allowing people to read what's in them but not make and save changes — or hidden from others entirely.

➡ Set up user accounts so that different users on a single computer access their own settings. Also, use parental controls so folks with more experience can guide those who are younger as they explore what the computer and Internet have to offer.

Get ready to . . .

Change the Windows Password

1. Choose Start➪Control Panel and then click User Accounts and Family Safety.

2. In the resulting window shown in Figure 14-1, click the Change Your Windows Password link. Then, if you have more than one user account, click an account to add the password to. Click the Create a Password for Your Account link.

3. In the Create a Password for Your Account screen, as shown in Figure 14-2, enter a password, confirm it, and add a password hint.

4. Click the Create Password button.

5. You return to the User Accounts window. If you wish to remove your password at some point, you can click the Remove Your Password link here.

6. Click the Close button to close the User Accounts window.

 If you forget your password, Windows shows the hint you entered to help you remember it, but remember that anybody who uses your computer can see the hint when it's displayed. So, if lots of people know that you drive a Ford and your hint is "My car model," your password-protection is about as effective as a thin raincoat in a hurricane.

 After you create a password, you can go to the User Accounts window and change it at any time by clicking Change Your Password. You can also change the name on your user account by clicking Change Your Name.

Figure 14-1: The User Accounts and Family Safety window

Figure 14-2: The Create a Password for Your Account screen

Allow Access to the Public Folder

1. Choose Start⇨Control Panel⇨Network and Internet.

2. In the resulting Network and Internet window, click Network and Sharing Center. In the resulting Network and Sharing Center dialog box, click the Change Advanced Sharing Settings link on the left. In the Public Folder Sharing section of this dialog box (see Figure 14-3), you can allow access with the ability to make changes, allow access without the ability to make changes, or not allow access.

3. Click Save Changes to save the setting and then click the Close button to close the Control Panel.

 The Public folder is found with the path `C:\Users\Public`. This is a handy way to share files on a network when you've protected your private folders.

 Even if you allow access to a printer through printer sharing, you may need to install that printer's drivers in each computer that accesses it. See Chapter 10 for more about setting up printers.

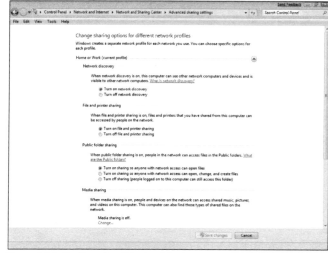

Figure 14-3: The Network and Sharing dialog box

Set Up Shared Folders

1. Locate the folder that you want to share by using Windows Explorer. (Right-click the Start button and choose Open Windows Explorer from the shortcut menu that appears.)

2. Right-click the folder that you want to allow others to access and then choose Share With. On the submenu that appears, choose Specific People (see Figure 14-4).

3. In the resulting File Sharing dialog box, as shown in Figure 14-5, click the arrow in the box to select users to share with and then click Add. To create a new user, choose Create a New User from the drop-down list that appears.

4. Click Share. A dialog box appears showing the progress; when the sharing is done, you see a message that your file is now shared.

5. Click Done to complete the file sharing process.

 To find out more about using Windows Explorer to locate and work with files, see Chapter 3.

 You can choose to share individual files by following the procedure outlined here, but if you change your mind, you can also remove permissions. To change the permissions for sharing a file with a particular user, display the File Sharing dialog box, click the name of a user, and choose Remove from the menu that appears.

Figure 14-4: Sharing a file from Windows Explorer

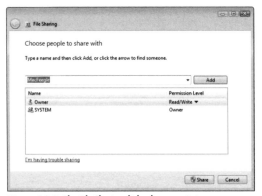

Figure 14-5: The File Sharing dialog box permissions

Set File Attributes

1. Locate the file that you want to modify by using Windows Explorer. (Right-click Start and choose Open Windows Explorer.)

2. Right-click the file and choose Properties.

3. In the resulting *Filename* Properties dialog box, as shown in Figure 14-6, click the General tab.

4. Select the Read-Only or Hidden check boxes.

5. Click OK to accept the new settings.

 If you want to see the files that you've marked as hidden, go to the file or folder location (for example, in the My Documents folder or by using Windows Explorer) and choose Organize➪Folder and Search Options. Click the View tab to display it, select the Show Hidden Files, Folders, and Drives radio button in the Advanced Settings and then click OK. Be aware that this reveals all hidden folders, not a particular folder.

 One other item you can change settings for in the Properties dialog box is how the navigation pane works in Windows Explorer. You can choose to Automatically Expand to Current Folder if you want, for example, to have the Documents folder always expanded when you open Windows Explorer.

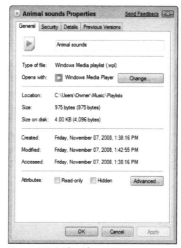

Figure 14-6: The *Filename* Properties dialog box

Create a New User Account

1. Choose Start⇨Control Panel.

2. In the resulting window, click the Add or Remove User Accounts link.

3. In the resulting Manage Accounts dialog box, as shown in Figure 14-7, click Create a New Account.

4. In the next dialog box, as shown in Figure 14-8, enter an account name and then select the type of account you want to create:

   • **Administrator,** who can do things like create and change accounts and install programs

   • **Standard user,** who can't do the tasks an administrator can

5. Click the Create Account button and then close the Control Panel.

 After you create an account, you can make changes to it, such as assigning a password or changing the account type, by double-clicking it in the Manage Accounts window you reached in Step 4 (in the preceding step list) and following the links listed there.

Figure 14-7: Creating a new user account

Figure 14-8: Choosing the account type

Switch User Accounts

1. Click Start and then click the arrow on the side of the Shut Down button (see Figure 14-9).

2. Choose Switch User. In the resulting window, click the user you want to log in as.

3. If the user account is password-protected, a box appears for you to enter the password. Type the password and then click the arrow button to log in.

4. Windows logs you in with the specified user's settings.

 If you don't like the picture associated with your user account, you can change it. Choose Start⇨Control Panel⇨Add or Remove User Accounts and then click the account you want to change. In the resulting window, click Change Your Account Picture and choose another picture or browse to see more picture choices.

 If you forget your password and try to switch users without entering one, Windows shows your password hint, which you can set when you initially choose your password.

Figure 14-9: Switching users

 You can set up several user accounts for your computer, which helps you save and access specific user settings and provide privacy for each user's files with passwords. To find out about setting up user accounts and changing their settings, see earlier tasks in this chapter.

Set Up Parental Controls

1. Choose Start➪Control Panel➪Set Up Parental Controls for Any User. In the resulting Parental Controls window (see Figure 14-10), click the user for whom you wish to apply Parental Controls.

2. In the resulting User Controls dialog box (see Figure 14-11), select the On, Enforce Current Settings check box to turn on Parental Controls.

3. Click any of the settings (Time Limits, Games, Allow and Block Specific Programs) to further control how much time can be spent online and what kinds of activities the user can engage in.

4. Click OK and then click the Close button to close the Parental Controls window. The settings take effect the next time the user logs in. If the user is currently logged in, the settings won't take place until he logs off and then logs on again or you restart the computer.

 Additional tools for filtering Web content are available in Internet Explorer 8 in an InPrivate Filtering add-on program. Visit Microsoft's Web site (www.microsoft.com) and search for InPrivate Filtering for more about this feature. Also see Chapter 7 for more about IE settings and features.

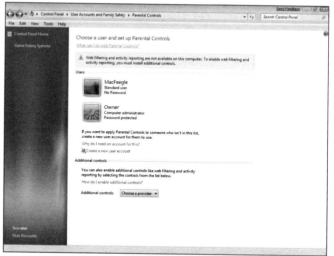

Figure 14-10: The Parental Controls window

Figure 14-11: The User Controls dialog box

Protecting Windows

Microsoft provides security features within Windows that help to keep your information private, whether at work or home, and also keep you in safe territory when you're online. You can do the following:

➠ **Set up Internet Explorer zones.** Designate Trusted Web sites (from which you feel perfectly safe downloading files) and Restricted sites (which are likely to contain things that you wouldn't download to your worst enemy's computer).

➠ **Make sure protections are up to date.** By enabling a firewall to keep your computer safe from outsiders and also keeping Windows up to date, you can avoid several kinds of attacks on your data. Windows can also let you know whether a computer you're using is protected by an antivirus program.

Chapter

15

Get ready to . . .

Set Up Trusted and Restricted Web Sites

1. Click the Internet Explorer icon in the left side of the Windows taskbar to start your browser.

2. Choose Tools⇨Internet Options.

3. In the Internet Options dialog box, click the Security tab (see Figure 15-1).

4. Click the Trusted Sites icon and then click the Sites button.

5. In the resulting Trusted Sites dialog box, enter a URL in the Add This Web Site to the Zone text box for a Web site you want to allow your computer to access.

6. Click Add to add the site to the list of Web sites, as shown in Figure 15-2.

7. Repeat Steps 3–6 to add more sites.

8. When you're done, click Close and then click OK to close the dialog boxes.

9. Repeat Steps 1–7, clicking the Restricted Sites icon rather than Trusted Sites in Step 4 to designate sites that you don't want your computer to access. Click the Apply button after each change.

 You can establish a privacy setting on the Privacy tab of the Internet Options dialog box to control which sites are allowed to download cookies to your computer. *Cookies* are tiny files that a site uses to track your online activity and recognize you when you return to the source site. *Trusted sites* are ones that you allow to download cookies to your computer even though the privacy setting you have made might not allow many other sites to do so. *Restricted sites* can never download cookies to your computer, no matter what your privacy setting is.

Figure 15-1: The Internet Options dialog box, Security tab

Figure 15-2: The Trusted Sites dialog box

 If the Require Server Verification (`https:`) for All Sites in This Zone check box is selected in the Trusted Sites dialog box, any Trusted site you add must use the `https` prefix, which indicates that the site has a secure connection.

Enable the Windows Firewall

1. Choose Start➪Control Panel➪System and Security➪ Windows Firewall.

2. In the Windows Firewall window that appears (see Figure 15-3), check that the Windows Firewall is marked as On. If it isn't, click the Turn Windows Firewall On or Off link in the left pane of the window.

3. In the resulting Customize Settings window (see Figure 15-4), select the Turn on Windows Firewall radio button for Home or Work (Private) Network Location Settings and/or Public Network Location Settings and then click OK.

4. Click the Close button to close the Windows Security Center and the Control Panel.

 A *firewall* is a program that protects your computer from the outside world. This is generally a good thing, unless you use a Virtual Private Network (VPN). Using a firewall with a VPN results in your being unable to share files and use some other VPN features.

 Antivirus and security software programs may offer their own firewall protection and may display a message asking whether you want to switch. Check their features against Windows and then decide, but usually most firewall features are comparable. The important thing is to have one activated.

Figure 15-3: The Windows Firewall window

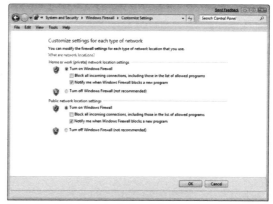

Figure 15-4: The Customize Settings dialog box

Allow a Program through the Firewall

1. Choose Start➪Control Panel➪System and Security➪ Allow a Program through Windows Firewall.

2. In the resulting Allowed Programs dialog box (see Figure 15-5), select the check box(es) for the program(s) you want to allow through the firewall and use the check boxes for Home/Work (Private) and Public to choose which type of network to allow the program(s) through.

3. Click OK to accept the settings. If you want to remove a program from the Allowed list in future, simply return to this dialog box, click the program in the list, and then click Remove.

 If you want to exclude certain networks from the firewall settings, from the Windows Firewall window (Control Panel➪System and Security➪Windows Firewall) make changes to settings for any network listed.

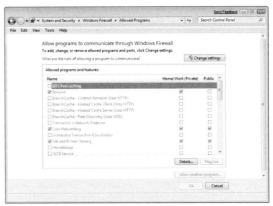

Figure 15-5: The Allowed Programs dialog box

Check Your Computer's Security Status

1. Choose Start➪Control Panel➪System and Security.

2. In the resulting System and Security window (see Figure 15-6), click the Review Your Computer's Status and Resolve Issues link.

3. In the Action Center window that appears (see Figure 15-7), check to see whether the Security item states whether Windows found any antivirus software on your computer.

4. If Windows didn't find such software, click the Find a Program Online button and review the recommended security software partners that Microsoft recommends. If you want to purchase one of these solutions, click the logo of the company you want to buy from and then you're taken to their site where you can buy and download the software.

It's very important that you have antivirus and antispyware software installed on your computer, and that you run updates to them on a regular basis. These types of programs help you avoid downloading malware to your computer that could cause advertising pop-ups, slow your computer's performance, damage computer files, track your keystrokes while you type to steal your identity, and more. If you don't want to pay for such a program, consider a free solution, such as Spyware Terminator (www.spyware terminator.com).

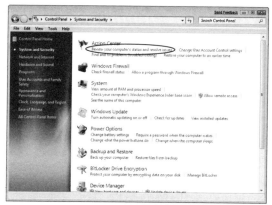

Figure 15-6: The System and Security window

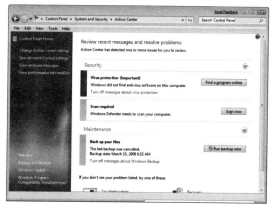

Figure 15-7: The Action Center window

Run a Windows Defender Scan

1. Choose Start⇨Control Panel⇨System and Security⇨ Review Your Computer's Status and Resolve Issues.

2. In the resulting Action Center window, click the Scan Now button for Windows Defender (see Figure 15-8).

3. The scan begins immediately, and a progress screen appears (see Figure 15-9). When the scan is complete, Windows Defender displays the results.

 Run a scan of your system on a regular basis. Windows Defender is set up by default to run a quick scan once a day. You can also use the method described here to run scans more often, or if you visit a site by mistake that you think could download malware to your computer.

Figure 15-8: The Windows Action Center

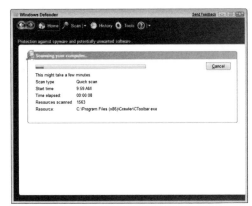

Figure 15-9: A scan in progress

Run Windows Update

1. Choose Start➪All Programs➪Windows Update.

2. In the Windows Update window, click Check for Updates. Windows thinks about this for a while, so feel free to page through a magazine for a minute or two.

3. In the resulting window, as shown in Figure 15-10, click the link indicating the number of updates available to view them.

4. In the following window, which shows the available updates (see Figure 15-11), click to select available critical or optional updates that you want to install. Then click OK.

5. In the Windows Update window that appears, click the Install Updates button. A window appears showing the progress of your installation. When the installation is complete, you might get a message telling you that it's a good idea to restart your computer to complete the installation. Click Restart Now.

 You can set up Windows Update to run at the same time every day. Click the Change Settings link in the Windows Update window and choose the frequency (such as Every Day) and time of day to check for and install updates.

 Running Windows Update either automatically or manually on a regular basis ensures that you get the latest security updates to the operating system, so it's a good idea to stay current.

Figure 15-10: The Windows Update window

Figure 15-11: Selecting which updates to install

Maintaining Windows

Chapter 16

*T*his chapter covers tasks akin to changing the oil in your car: Maintenance might not be a barrel of laughs, but it keeps your car (or in this case, your computer) running, so it has to be done. These are the types of tasks that help you organize, maintain, and protect your computer system.

Windows 7 handles lots and lots of files. To keep your computer and Windows in tip-top shape, you need to organize files in logical ways, perform maintenance activities, prepare for disaster — and know how to recover from it.

The tasks in this chapter fall into three different categories:

➡ **Backing up your files:** Backing up files is a good computing practice, guaranteeing that you have a copy of all your work in case of a crash. You have to use a writable CD or DVD disc to back up files to it.

➡ **Performing basic maintenance:** These tasks are the equivalent of a janitorial service. To keep your system in shape, you can *defragment* your hard drive (take little fragments of files and consolidate them for efficiency) or free up space on the drive. These two tasks troubleshoot files on your hard drive to make sure that you get the best performance from your computer.

➡ **Clearing up clutter:** You can delete temporary files placed on your computer during online sessions to stop them from cluttering your hard drive. You can also schedule routine maintenance tasks to happen automatically so you don't take a chance that you forget to perform them.

Get ready to . . .

Back Up Files to a Writable CD or DVD

1. Place a blank writable CD-R/RW (read/writable) or DVD-R/RW in your CD-ROM or DVD-ROM drive and then choose Start➪Documents.

2. In the resulting Documents window (see Figure 16-1), select all the files that you want to copy to disc.

3. Right-click the files that you want and then choose Copy to Folder.

4. In the Copy Items dialog box that appears, click the CD-ROM or DVD-ROM drive and click Copy.

5. Click the Close button to close the Document window.

 If you want to back up the entire contents of a folder, such as the Documents folder, you can just click the Documents folder itself in Step 2.

 You can also back up to a network or another drive by using the Back Up Your Computer link in the Control Panel. With Windows Backup, you can make settings to regularly back up to a local disk or a CD-ROM or DVD-ROM drive, or to a network. Backing up to a CD/DVD is a little different from burning a disc in that after you back up your files, only changes are saved each subsequent time a backup is run.

Figure 16-1: Files selected for copying in the Documents window

Defragment a Hard Drive

1. Choose Start⇨Control Panel⇨System and Security and then click Defragment Your Hard Drive in the Administrative Tools.

2. In the resulting Disk Defragmenter window (see Figure 16-2), to the left of the Defragment Disk button is the Analyze Disk button. Use this to check whether your disk requires defragmenting. When the analysis is complete, click the Defragment Disk button. A notation appears (see Figure 16-3) showing the progress of defragmenting your drive.

3. When the defragmenting process is complete, the Disk Defragmenter window shows that your drive no longer requires defragmenting. Click Close to close the window.

 Warning: Disk defragmenting could take a while. If you have energy-saving features active (such as a screen saver), they could cause the defragmenter to stop and start all over again. Try running your defrag overnight while you're happily dreaming of much more interesting things. You can also set up the procedure to run automatically at a preset period of time when your computer is on but you're away from it, such as once every two weeks, by using the Run Automatically setting in the Disk Defragmenter window.

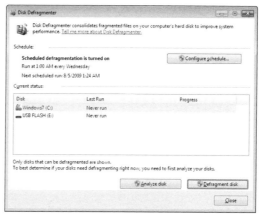

Figure 16-2: The Disk Defragmenter window

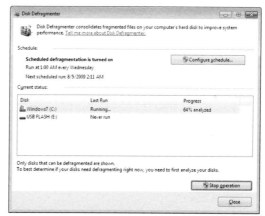

Figure 16-3: The Disk Defragmenter in action

Free Disk Space

1. Choose Start⇨Control Panel⇨System and Security and then click Free Up Disk Space in the Administrative Tools.

2. In the Disk Cleanup dialog box that appears (see Figure 16-4), if you have more than one drive, choose the drive you want to clean up from the drop-down list and click OK.

3. The resulting dialog box shown in Figure 16-5 tells you that Disk Cleanup calculated how much space can be cleared on your hard drive and displays the suggested files to delete in a list (those to be deleted have a check mark next to them). If you want to select additional files in the list to delete, click to place a check mark next to them.

4. After you select all the files to delete, click OK. The selected files are deleted.

 Click the View Files button in the Disk Cleanup dialog box to see more details about the files that Windows proposes to delete, including the size of the files and when they were created or last accessed.

 If you can't free up enough disk space for your needs, you might want to replace your hard drive with one that has more capacity.

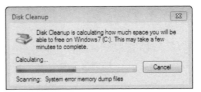

Figure 16-4: Choose the drive to clean up

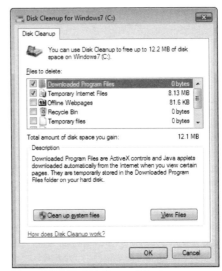

Figure 16-5: The Disk Cleanup dialog box

Delete Temporary Internet Files by Using Internet Explorer

1. Open Internet Explorer.

2. Choose Tools⇨Internet Options.

3. On the General tab of the resulting Internet Options dialog box (see Figure 16-6), click the Delete button in the Browsing History section.

4. In the resulting Delete Browsing History dialog box, as shown in Figure 16-7, select the Temporary Internet Files check box to select it if it's not already selected and then click Delete.

5. A confirmation message asks whether you want to delete the files. Click Yes. Click Close and then click OK to close the open dialog boxes.

 Temporary Internet files can be deleted when you run Disk Cleanup (see the "Free Disk Space" task earlier in this chapter), but the process that I describe here allows you to delete them without having to make choices about deleting other files on your system.

 Windows 7 offers a feature for rating and improving your computer's performance. From the Control Panel, click System and Security and then click the Check Your Computer's Windows Experience Index Base Score link. In the resulting dialog box, click the Rate This Computer button to get a rating of your processor speed, memory operations, and more.

Figure 16-6: The Internet Options dialog box

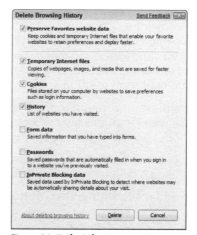

Figure 16-7: The Delete Browsing History dialog box

Schedule Maintenance Tasks

1. Choose Start➪Control Panel➪System and Security and then click Schedule Tasks in the Administrative Tools.

2. In the resulting Task Scheduler dialog box, as shown in Figure 16-8, choose Action➪Create Task.

3. In the resulting Create Task dialog box (see Figure 16-9), enter a task name and description. Choose when to run the task (only when you're logged on, or whether you're logged on or not).

4. Click the Triggers tab and then click New. In the New Trigger dialog box, choose a criterion in the Begin the Task drop-down list and use the settings to specify how often to perform the task as well as when and at what time of day to begin. Click OK.

5. Click the Actions tab and then click New. In the New Action dialog box, choose the action that will occur from the Action drop-down list. These include starting a program, sending an e-mail, or displaying a message. Depending on what you choose here, different action dialog boxes appear. For example, if you want to send an e-mail, you get an e-mail form to fill in.

6. If you want to set conditions in addition to those that trigger the action, click the Conditions tab and enter them.

7. In the resulting dialog box, select a start time and start date by clicking the arrows in each field and then click Next.

8. Click the Settings tab and make settings that control how the task runs.

9. After you complete all settings, click OK to save the task.

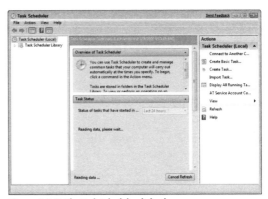

Figure 16-8: The Task Scheduler dialog box

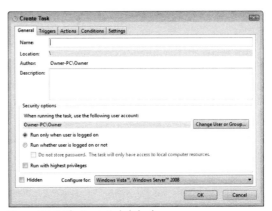

Figure 16-9: The Create Task dialog box

 If you like a more wizard-like interface for building a new task, you can choose the Create Basic Task item from the Actions menu. This walks you through the most basic and minimal settings you can make to create a new task.

Part VI
Fixing Common Problems

The 5th Wave — By Rich Tennant

"How's the defragmentation coming?"

Troubleshooting Hardware Problems

Computer hardware, like your CPU and printer, is cool. *Hardware* is the gadgetry that hums and beeps and looks neat on your desktop. But when hardware goes wrong, you might be tempted to throw it out the window. Don't do that — think of all the money you spent on it. Instead, use Windows to isolate and troubleshoot the problem.

Windows has several features that help you diagnose and treat the sickest hardware, including

➡ A method of checking whether your printer model is compatible with Windows 7

➡ A Disk Cleanup feature that checks your hard drive for problems that could be causing poor performance, such as bad sectors on the drive or bits of stray data that could simply be thrown away — and then frees space and helps your system to perform better

➡ A Hardware Troubleshooter feature in the Windows Help and Support Center that offers advice to help you fix a variety of hardware problems

➡ The ability to quickly and easily update hardware drivers that might help your hardware perform optimally or revert to a previous driver if a newer version is causing problems

Run Error Checking to Detect Bad Sectors on a Hard Drive

1. Choose Start⇨Computer.

2. Right-click the drive you want to repair and then choose Properties.

3. In the resulting Properties dialog box, click the Tools tab to display it (see Figure 17-1) and then click the Check Now button.

4. In the resulting Check Disk dialog box (see Figure 17-2), choose the option you want to use:

   • **Automatically Fix File System Errors:** You have to close all files in order to run this option.

   • **Scan For and Attempt Recovery of Bad Sectors:** If you select this option, it also automatically fixes any errors found, so you don't need to select the first option as well.

Figure 17-1: The Properties dialog box, Tools tab

5. Click Start.

 If unrecoverable sectors can't be fixed by using this utility, they're flagged so that Windows doesn't attempt to access them anymore.

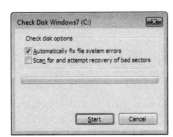

Figure 17-2: The Check Disk dialog box

Use the Hardware Troubleshooter

1. Choose Start⇨Control Panel⇨Find and Fix Problems (under System and Security).

2. In the resulting Troubleshooting window, click the Hardware and Sound link (see Figure 17-3).

3. Click the device you want help with. (For example, if your audio isn't working, click the Playing Audio link or if you're having trouble with a printer or other device, click Hardware and Devices.) Follow the instructions to allow Windows to detect and attempt to fix to your problem. (Figure 17-4 shows the results of the Hardware and Devices troubleshooting, for example.)

4. After you determine that Windows has solved the problem, click the Close button to close the Troubleshooting window. If you don't find a solution, consider using the Remote Assistance feature to get one-on-one help (see Chapter 19 for more about this feature).

 You can also look in the Help and Support feature for Troubleshooting features in topics lists. For example, under Printers and Printing, you'll find a Troubleshoot Printers or Printing Problems topic.

 If the procedure didn't fix the problem, click the Explore Additional Options link in the final Troubleshooter dialog box. This takes you to a list of various Help options.

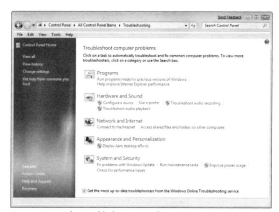

Figure 17-3: The Troubleshooting window

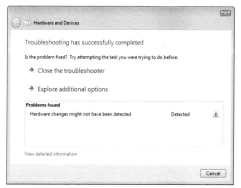

Figure 17-4: Troubleshooting results

Update a Driver

1. Be sure you're connected to the Internet and then choose Start➪Control Panel➪Hardware and Sound.

2. In the resulting Hardware and Sound window, click the Device Manager link.

3. In the resulting Device Manager window (see Figure 17-5), click a device category to display specific devices, and then right-click a device and choose Properties. In the Properties dialog box that appears, click the Driver tab (see Figure 17-6).

4. Click the Update Driver button. Windows searches for any updated driver that might be available. Click OK to close the Properties dialog box.

 In some cases, you have to reboot your computer to give Windows a chance to load the new driver. Choose Start➪Shut Down➪Restart. The driver should now, by the magic of the Windows Plug and Play feature that automatically detects new hardware, be working.

 If you don't find the updated driver by using the Windows 7 procedure outlined earlier, consider going directly to the hardware manufacturer's Web site and downloading the latest driver.

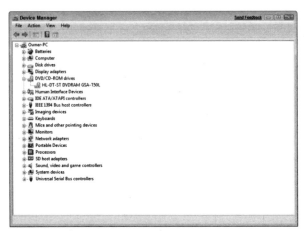

Figure 17-5: The Device Manager window

Figure 17-6: The Properties dialog box, Driver tab

Revert to a Previous Version of a Driver

1. Disconnect the device that's associated with the driver that's causing trouble.

2. Turn off the device.

3. Choose Start⇨Control Panel⇨Hardware and Sound and click the Device Manager link.

4. In the resulting Device Manager window, click a device category to display the devices, and then right-click the device you want to rollback and choose Properties.

5. In the resulting Properties window on the Drivers tab (see Figure 17-7), click the Roll Back Driver button and follow the instructions.

Figure 17-7: The Properties dialog box, Driver tab

 Another option if you've begun experiencing difficulties with your computer or piece of hardware is to do a System Restore. This restores settings to a previous date when things were working correctly. See Chapter 18 for more about this feature.

Troubleshooting Software Problems

*A*ll the wonderful hardware that you've spent your hard-earned money on doesn't mean a thing if the software driving it goes flooey. If any programs cause your system to *crash* (meaning it freezes up, and you have to take drastic measures to revive it), you can try a variety of tasks to fix it. In this chapter, you find out how to recover when the following problems occur:

➡ When a program crashes, you can simply shut down that program by using the Windows Task Manager. This utility keeps track of all the programs and processes that are running on your computer.

➡ If you have problems and Windows isn't responding, sometimes it helps to restart in Safe Mode, which requires only basic files and drivers. Restarting in Safe Mode often allows you to troubleshoot what's going on, and you can restart Windows in its regular mode after the problem's solved.

➡ Use the System Restore feature to first create a *system restore point* (a point in time when your settings and programs all seem to be humming along just fine) and then restore Windows to that point when trouble hits.

➡ If you need a little help, you might run a troubleshooting program to help you figure out a problem you're experiencing with a program.

Chapter 18

Get ready to . . .

Shut Down a Nonresponsive Application

1. Press Ctrl+Alt+Del.

2. In the Windows screen that appears, click Start Task Manager.

3. In the resulting Windows Task Manager dialog box (see Figure 18-1), select the application that you were in when your system stopped responding.

4. Click the End Task button.

5. In the resulting dialog box, the Windows Task Manager tells you that the application isn't responding and asks whether you want to shut it down now. Click Yes.

Figure 18-1: The Windows Task Manager dialog box

 If pressing Ctrl+Alt+Del doesn't bring up the Task Manager, you're in bigger trouble than you thought. You might need to press and hold your computer power button to shut down. Note that some applications use an AutoSave feature that keeps an interim version of the document that you're working in — you might be able to save some of your work by opening that last-saved version. Other programs don't have such a safety net, and you simply lose whatever changes you made to your document since the last time you saved it. The moral? Save, and save often.

 You may see a dialog box appear when an application shuts down that asks whether you want to report the problem to Microsoft. If you say yes, information is sent to the people at Microsoft to help them provide advice or fix the problem down the road.

Restart Windows in Safe Mode

1. Remove any CDs or DVDs from your computer.

2. Choose Start, click the arrow on the right of the Lock button, and then choose Restart to reboot your system (see Figure 18-2).

3. When the computer starts to reboot (the screen goes black), press F8.

4. If you have more than one operating system, you might see the Windows Advanced Options menu. Use the up- and down-arrow keys to select the Windows 7 operating system. Or, type the number of that choice, press Enter, and then continue to press F8.

5. In the resulting plain-vanilla text-based screen, press the up- or down-arrow key to choose the Safe Mode option from the list and then press Enter.

6. Log in to your computer with administrator privileges; a Safe Mode screen appears (see Figure 18-3). Use the tools in the Control Panel and the Help and Support system to figure out your problem, make changes, and then restart. When you restart again (repeat Step 2), let your computer start in the standard Windows 7 mode.

 When you reboot and press F8 as in Step 3, you're in the old text-based world that users of the DOS operating system will remember. It's scary out there! Your mouse doesn't work a lick, and no fun sounds or cool graphics exist to soothe you. In fact, DOS is the reason the whole *For Dummies* series started because *everybody* felt like a dummy using it, me included. Just use your arrow keys to get around and press Enter to make selections. You're back in Windows-land soon . . .

Figure 18-2: The Windows desktop in Safe Mode

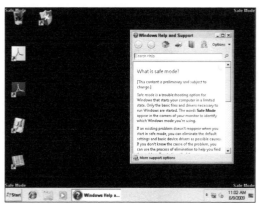

Figure 18-3: Windows 7 running in Safe Mode

Create a System Restore Point

1. You can back up your system files, which creates a restore point you can later use to return your computer to earlier settings if you begin to experience problems. Choose Start⇨Control Panel⇨System and Security and in the resulting System and Security dialog box, click the System link.

2. In the System dialog box, click the System Protection link in the left panel. In the System Properties dialog box that appears (see Figure 18-4), on the System Protection tab, click the Create button.

3. In the Create a Restore Point dialog box that appears, enter a name to identify the restore point, such as the current date or the name of a program you're about to install, and click Create.

4. Windows displays a progress window. When the restore point is created, the message shown in Figure 18-5 appears. Click Close to close the message box, and click Close to close the System Protection dialog box, and then click Close again to close the Control Panel.

 Every once in a while, when you install some software, make some new settings in Windows, and things seem to be running just fine, create a system restore point. It's good computer practice, just like backing up your files, only you're backing up your settings. Once a month or once every couple months works for most people, but if you frequently make changes, create a system restore point more often.

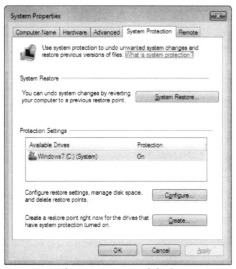

Figure 18-4: The System Protection dialog box, System Protection tab

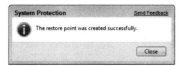

Figure 18-5: The Create a Restore Point confirmation dialog box

 A more drastic option to System Restore is to run the system recovery disc that probably came with your computer or that you created using discs you provided. However, system recovery essentially puts your computer right back to the configuration it had when it was carried out of the factory. In most cases, using system recovery discs means you lose any software you've installed and documents you've created since you began to use it. A good argument for creating system restore points on a regular basis, don't you think?

Restore the Windows System

1. Choose Start⇨Control Panel⇨Back Up Your Computer (under System and Security).

2. In the Back Up and Restore window, click the Recovery Control Panel link. In the Recovery window shown in Figure 18-6, click the Open System Restore button.

3. The System Restore feature shows a progress dialog box as it starts. In the resulting System Restore window, click Next.

4. In the System Restore dialog box that appears, click the system restore point to which you want to restore the computer and click the Next button.

5. A dialog box confirms that you want to run System Restore and informs you that your computer will need to restart to complete the process. Close any open files or programs, and then click Finish to proceed.

6. The system goes through a shutdown and restart sequence, and then displays a dialog box that informs you that the System Restore has occurred.

7. Click OK to close it.

 System Restore doesn't get rid of files that you've saved, so you don't lose your Ph.D. dissertation. System Restore simply reverts to Windows settings as of the restore point. This can help if you or some piece of installed software made a setting that's causing some conflict in your system that makes your computer sluggish or prone to crashes. If you're concerned about what changes will happen, click the Scan for Affected Programs button shown in the window displayed in Figure 18-7.

Figure 18-6: The Recovery window

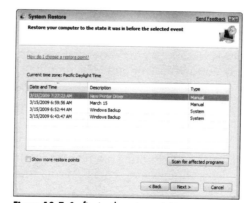

Figure 18-7: Confirming the restore point to use

 System Restore doesn't always solve the problem. Your very best bet is to be sure you create a set of backup discs for your computer when you buy it. If you didn't do that and you can't get things running right again, contact your computer manufacturer. They may be able to send you a set of recovery discs, though they may charge a small fee.

Troubleshoot Software Problems

1. Choose Start➪Control Panel➪Find and Fix Problems (under System and Security).

2. In the resulting Troubleshooting window (see Figure 18-8), click Programs.

3. In the resulting Troubleshooting Problems – Programs window (see Figure 18-9), choose what you want to troubleshoot:

   • **Network** allows you to troubleshoot a connection to the Internet.

   • **Web Browser** helps you figure out problems you may be having with the Internet Explorer browser.

   • **Program Compatibility** is a good choice if you have an older program that doesn't seem to be functioning well with this version of Windows. Program compatibility is a common cause of problems running software.

   • **Printing** allows you to find out why you're having difficulty with your printer, including checking for the correct printer driver software.

   • **Media Player** troubleshooting can be used to pinpoint problems with general settings, media files, or playing DVDs.

4. Follow the sequence of instructions for the item you selected to let Windows help you resolve your problem.

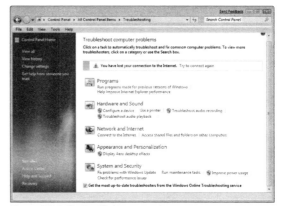

Figure 18-8: The Troubleshooting window

Figure 18-9: The Troubleshooting Problems – Programs window

In some cases, you'll be asked for administrator permission for the troubleshooter to perform an action, so it's a good idea to run the Troubleshooting Wizard through an administrator level account. See Chapter 14 for more about user accounts and administrators.

Getting Help

*W*ith so many Windows features, you're bound to run into something that doesn't work right or isn't easy to figure out (or that this book doesn't cover). That's when you need to call on the resources that Microsoft provides to help you.

Through the Help and Support Center, you can get help in various ways, including the following:

➥ **Access information that's stored in the Help system database.** Drill down from one topic to another or by using a powerful search mechanism. A troubleshooting feature even helps you pin down your problem.

➥ **Get help from your fellow Windows users.** Tap into information exchanged by users in Windows Communities or by using a little feature called *Remote Assistance*, which allows you to let another user take over your computer from a distance (via the Internet) and figure out your problem for you.

➥ **Bite the bullet and pay for it.** Microsoft offers some help for free (for example, help for installing its software that you paid good money for), but some help comes with a price. When you can't find help anywhere else, you might want to consider forking over a few hard-earned bucks for this option.

IIII➡ **Chapter**
19

Get ready to . . .

Explore the Help Table of Contents

1. Choose Start➪Help and Support to open Windows Help and Support, as shown in Figure 19-1. *Note:* If your copy of Windows came built into your computer, some computer manufacturers (such as Hewlett-Packard), customize this center to add information that's specific to your computer system.

2. Click the Browse Help Topics link to display a list of topics. Click any of the topics to see a list of subtopics. Eventually, you get down to the deepest level of detailed subtopics, as shown in Figure 19-2.

3. Click a subtopic to read its contents. Some subtopics contain blue links that lead to related topics or perform an action, such as opening a dialog box. Green links display a definition or explanation of a term when clicked.

4. When you finish reading a Help topic, click the Close button to close the Help and Support window.

 You can click the Print icon in the set of tools at the top right of the Help and Support window to print any displayed topic. You can also click the Restore Down button in the title bar to minimize the window and keep it available while you work in your computer.

 Windows will automatically get the most up to date Help information if you're connected to the Internet when you open Help and Support. If you're not connected, you can still browse the database of Help information installed with Windows 7.

Figure 19-1: The Windows Help and Support window

Figure 19-2: Detailed level Help subtopics

Search for Help

1. Open Windows Help and Support by choosing Start⇨ Help and Support.

2. Enter a search term in the Search box and then click the Search Help button (the little magnifying glass icon on the right side of the Search box). Search results, such as those shown in Figure 19-3, appear.

3. Explore topics by clicking various links in the search results. These links offer a few different types of help:

   • Some of the results are procedures, such as "Make the mouse easier to use."

   • Troubleshooting help items are phrased as statements, such as "I can't hear any text read aloud with Narrator." Clicking one of these items takes you to a troubleshooter wizard.

   • Some items provide general information rather than procedures, such as "Tips for Searching the Internet" (see Figure 19-4).

4. If you have no luck, enter a different search term in the Search text box and start again.

 If you don't find what you need with Search, consider clicking the Browse Help button in the top right of the Help and Support window (it sports a little blue icon in the shape of a book) to display a list of major topics. Those topics may also give you some ideas for good search terms to continue your search.

Figure 19-3: The result of a search for the keyword *mouse*

Figure 19-4: An article displayed from a search

Post a Question in Windows Communities

1. Open Windows Help and Support (see "Explore the Help Table of Contents," earlier in the chapter). Click the Ask button in the top-right corner. In the Ask a Person for Help section of the page, click the Windows Communities link.

2. In the Microsoft Windows TechNet page that opens in your browser, click the Community tab (see Figure 19-5).

3. Click a topic link, which displays the discussion summary and indicates the number of discussion threads and messages (see Figure 19-6).

4. Click the discussion title to display the threads contained in it.

5. Click a thread title to open it, scroll through the original posting, and reply to it.

   - **Post a new message.** To post a message, you have to sign into Microsoft TechNet with a Windows Live ID (which you can get for free by going to www.windows live.com). Next, select the discussion group to participate in and then click the Ask a Question button. If you've never participated in a discussion, you're asked to create a profile. Enter a display name and click the Accept button. In the Start a New Question or Discussion form, enter the Title and message Body in their respective text boxes. Add any descriptive tags or categories, and then click Submit to post your question.

   - **Reply to a message in a discussion.** With the list of postings and replies displayed, click the Reply button, fill in the message, and then click Post.

Figure 19-5: The Windows 7 TechNet Community page

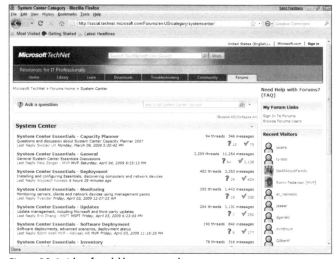

Figure 19-6: A list of available community discussions

Access Windows Online Help

1. Open Windows Help and Support and then click the Windows Website link.

2. In the window that appears (see Figure 19-7), click the Getting Started link. In the Getting Started window that appears, click the Windows Basics link. In the Windows Basics window (see Figure 19-8), click any topic listed to get further help.

3. Click the Close button to close the online Help window in your browser and then click the Close button to close Windows Help and Support.

 To set up Help and Support to always include Windows Online Help and Support when you search for Help, click the Options button and choose Settings. Be sure the Improve My Search Results by Using Online Help (Recommended) check box is selected.

Figure 19-7: The Windows 7 Online Help page

Figure 19-8: An online FAQ topic

Connect to Remote Assistance

1. Enable Remote Assistance by choosing Start⇨Control Panel⇨System and Security⇨System⇨Remote Settings. On the Remote tab of the System Properties dialog box that's displayed, select the Allow Remote Assistance Connections to This Computer check box and then click OK.

2. Open Windows Help and Support.

3. Click the Ask button and then click the Windows Remote Assistance link. On the window that appears, as shown in Figure 19-9, click the Invite Someone You Trust to Help You link.

4. On the page that appears, you can choose to use your e-mail to invite somebody to help you. You have two options:

   • Click the Send This Invitation as a File link and follow the instructions to save it as a file; then you can attach it to a message by using your Web-based e-mail program.

   • Click the Use E-mail to Send an Invitation link to use a pre-configured e-mail program to send an e-mail (see Figure 19-10). Enter an address and additional message content, if you like, and send the e-mail.

5. In the Windows Remote Assistance window, as shown in Figure 19-11, note the provided password.

6. When an incoming connection is made, use the tools there to adjust settings, chat, send a file, or pause, cancel, or stop sharing.

7. When you're finished, click the Close button to close the Windows Remote Assistance window.

8. If you want to require a password, enter it and confirm it.

Figure 19-9: The Windows Remote Assistance page

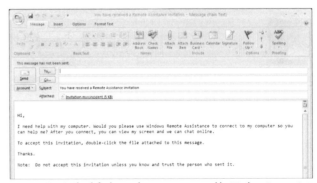

Figure 19-10: The default e-mail invitation generated by Windows Remote Assistance

Figure 19-11: The Windows Remote Assistance password

Change Help and Support Center Display Options

1. Open Windows Help and Support.

2. Choose Options⇨Text Size and then choose one of the text size options: Largest, Larger, Medium (the default), Smaller, or Smallest (see Figure 19-12).

3. Your new settings take effect immediately; click the Close button or navigate to another area of the Help and Support Center.

 If you don't like the colors in your Help and Support screen, you can change them by choosing a different color scheme in the Control Panel, Appearance and Personalization settings.

 Don't forget that you can reduce the size of the display by clicking the Restore Down button in the upper-right corner of the window. This is especially useful with the Help window so you can display it side by side with an application or Control Panel window in which you're trying to troubleshoot the described Help topic.

Figure 19-12: The Help and Support Center Options menu

Contact Microsoft Customer Support

1. Go to Windows Help and Support and click the Ask button in the upper-right corner. On the page that appears, as shown in Figure 19-13, click the Microsoft Customer Support link to open the Customer Support Web site in your default browser.

2. In the Windows Help and Support window that appears, click a product to see what support options and information are offered (see Figure 19-14).

3. Click various links for Help topics. If you need help with Downloads and Updates, or Installation and Setup, click those links along the left side of the product window.

4. Click the E-mail or Search links along the left to contact Microsoft or search for online Help topics.

5. Click the Close button to close the Internet Explorer browser.

 Typically, you can call support for two free help sessions or unlimited installation support by submitting a request via e-mail support or calling 1-800-936-3500. There is the option of Premier Third Tier Support, but this is for what Microsoft refers to as *non–mission critical* issues. This program is geared towards corporations and gives customers access to Microsoft experts to solve their problems.

 To find out about specific support options in your country, click the Understand Your Support Options link in the Help and Support home page. Click Support Options on the page that appears, select your country, and press Enter. Use the product finder feature to drill down to the specific help available to you.

Figure 19-13: The Microsoft Customer Support link

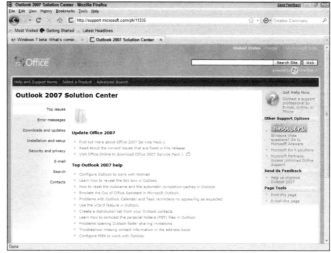

Figure 19-14: A variety of customer support options

Part VII
Fun and Games

The 5th Wave   By Rich Tennant

"I finally mastered all the game levels and thought
I'd set up a blacksmith shop and sell swords.
Two days later, a Wal-Mart goes up just
outside the village square."

Playing Games in Windows 7

All work and no play is just wrong no matter how you look at it. So, Microsoft has built plenty of games into Windows to keep you amused.

Many computer games are essentially virtual versions of games that you already know, such as Solitaire and Chess. But Windows has added some interesting treats to the mix — several that depend to a great extent on some neat onscreen animation.

Altogether, you can access nine games through Windows, and this chapter gives you a sampling of the best of them. Here's what you can expect:

➡ Traditional card games, such as Solitaire and Hearts

➡ Games of dexterity, such as Minesweeper, in which the goal is to be the fastest, smartest clicker in the West

➡ A game that's great for small children — Purble Place — in which the object is to place features on a cartoon character's face that match up

This chapter also covers setting up a gaming joystick as well as selecting a game rating system that allows you to pick and choose the games you want your family to play.

Chapter

20

Get ready to . . .

Play Solitaire

1. Choose Start⇨Games. If this is the first time you're playing games, Windows displays a Set Up Game Updates and Options dialog box. If it does, make choices (such as whether to automatically check for game updates) and click OK. In the resulting Games window, (see Figure 20-1), double-click Solitaire.

2. In the resulting Solitaire window, click a card (see Figure 20-2) and then click a card in another deck that you want to move it on top of. The first card you click moves.

3. When playing the game, you have these options:

   • If no moves are available, click the stack of cards in the upper-left corner to deal another round of cards.

   • If you move the last card from one of the six laid-out stacks, leaving only face-down cards, click the face-down cards to flip up one. You can also move a King onto any empty stack.

   • When you reach the end of the stack of cards in the upper-left corner, click them again to re-deal the cards that you didn't use the first time.

   • You can play a card in one of two places: either building a stack from King to Ace on the bottom row, alternating suits; or starting from Ace in any of the top four slots, placing cards from Ace to King in a single suit.

   • When you complete a set of cards (Ace to King), click the top card and then click one of the four blank deck spots at the top-right of the window. If you complete all four sets, you win.

4. To close Solitaire, click the Close button.

Figure 20-1: The Games window

Figure 20-2: The Solitaire game window

 To deal a new game, choose Game⇨New Game (or click F2). Unlike life, it's easy to start over with Solitaire!

Play FreeCell

1. Choose Start⇨Games; in the Games window, double-click FreeCell.

2. In the resulting FreeCell window, as shown in Figure 20-3, a game is ready to play. If you want a fresh game, you can always choose Game⇨New Game; a new game is dealt and ready to play.

 The goal is to move all the cards, grouped by the four suits, to the home cells (the four cells in the upper-right corner) stacked in order from Ace at the bottom to King at the top. The trick here is that you get four free cells (the four cells in the upper-left corner) where you can manually move a card out of the way to free up a move. You can also use those four slots to allow you to move up to four cards in a stack at once. (For example, if you want to move a Jack, 10, 9, and 8 all together onto a Queen.) You can move only as many cards as there are free cells available plus one. Free spaces in the rows of card stacks also act as free cells. You win when you have four stacks of cards for each of the four suits placed on the home cells.

3. Click a card; to move it, click a free cell or another card at the bottom of a column. Figure 20-4 shows a game where two free cells are already occupied.

 If you move a card to a free cell, you can move it back to the bottom of a column, but only on a card one higher in an alternate color. You could move a 3 of hearts to a 4 of spades, for example. You stack the cards in the columns in alternating colors, but the cards in the home cells end up in order and all in one suit.

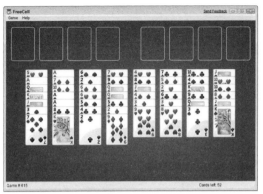

Figure 20-3: A new FreeCell game

Figure 20-4: Occupied cells

 If you get hooked on this game, try going to `www.freecell.org`, a Web site devoted to FreeCell. Here you can engage in live games with other players, read more about the rules and strategies, and even buy FreeCell merchandise. Don't say I didn't warn you about the possibility of addiction.

Play Spider Solitaire

1. Choose Start⇨Games; in the Games window, double-click Spider Solitaire. If you've never played the game before, the Select Difficulty window appears. Click your comfort level: Beginner, Intermediate, or Advanced.

2. In the resulting game window, click a card and then click another card or drag it to the bottom of another stack or to an empty stack so that you match the same suit in each stack, moving in descending order from King to Ace (see Figure 20-5).

3. Move a card to automatically turn over a new card in the stack.

4. After you complete a set of cards in a suit, those cards are moved off the game area. The goal is to remove all the cards in the fewest moves. You can

   - **Deal a new set of cards.** Choose Game⇨New Game or click the stack of cards in the bottom-right corner to deal a new set of cards. (*Note:* You have to have a card on each of the ten stacks before you can deal new ones.)

   - **Save your game.** Choose Game⇨Exit and then click Save in the Exit Game dialog box to save your game.

   - **Change the options.** Choose Game⇨Options (see Figure 20-6) and select a new difficulty level. Other options mainly affect how or whether you save games and open them to continue, and whether the various annoying or angelic sounds play when you click a card, deal a card, or fold a stack.

5. When you finish playing, click the Close button and either click Save or Don't Save in the Exit Game dialog box.

Figure 20-5: The Spider Solitaire game window

Figure 20-6: The Spider Options dialog box

 Stuck for a move? Try choosing Game⇨Hint. Various combinations of cards are highlighted in sequence to suggest a likely next step in the game. If you're not stuck but just bored with the appearance of the game, choose Game⇨Change Appearance and select another desk and background style.

Play Minesweeper

1. Choose Start⇨Games; in the Games window, double-click Minesweeper. If you've never played the game, a Select Difficulty dialog box appears. Click your selection.

2. The Minesweeper game board opens (see Figure 20-7). Click a square on the board, and a timer starts counting the seconds of your game.

   • If you click a square and a number appears, the number tells you how many mines are within the eight squares surrounding that square; if it remains blank, there are no mines within the eight squares surrounding it.

   • If you click a square and a bomb appears, all the hidden bombs are exposed (see Figure 20-8), and the game is over.

   • Right-click a square once to place a flag on it marking it as a mine. Right-click a square twice to place a question mark on it if you think it might contain a bomb to warn yourself to stay away for now.

3. To begin a new game, choose Game⇨New Game. In the New Game dialog box, click Quit and Start a New Game. If you want to play a game with the same settings as the previous one, click Restart This Game.

4. You can set several game options through the Game menu:

   • To change the expertise required, choose Game⇨Options and then choose Beginner, Intermediate, or Advanced.

   • To change the color of the playing board, choose Game⇨Change Appearance.

5. To end the game, click the Close button.

Figure 20-7: A new Minesweeper game

Figure 20-8: You lose!

 If you want a bigger game board (more squares, more bombs, more fun), choose Game⇨Options and then click Custom and specify the number of squares across and down and the number of bombs hidden within them.

 If you want to see how many games you've won, your longest winning or losing streak, and more, choose Game⇨Statistics.

Play Purble Place

1. Choose Start⇨Games; double-click Purble Place. If you're playing this for the first time, select a difficulty level in the resulting dialog box.

     Purble Place is actually made up of three games: Comfy Cakes, Purble Shop, and Purble Pairs. All are aimed at younger children to help them learn to match things, and all offer easy to follow pop-up instructions.

2. In the resulting Purble Place window (see Figure 20-9), click one of three items to begin a game:

    *   The schoolhouse opens Purble Pairs, in which you click two squares at a time, trying to find pairs of items.

    *   The bakery displays Comfy Cakes, in which you assemble a cake to match the picture.

    *   The Purble Shop contains a little character for whom you have to select the eyes, nose, and mouth that match.

3. In the game window (Figure 20-10 shows Comfy Cakes), follow the onscreen instructions to make selections. In Comfy Cakes, for example, click a cake shape and then click the large green arrow button on the screen to move the cake to the next station. Choose icing and decorations that match the picture of the cake on the TV.

4. To return to the main menu, choose Game⇨Main Menu and click Yes in the dialog box that appears. To exit the game entirely, click the Close button.

     A shortcut in each game window takes you back to the main menu. Click the little building icons (shop, school, and home) that are surrounded by a green arrow.

Figure 20-9: The Purble Place main menu

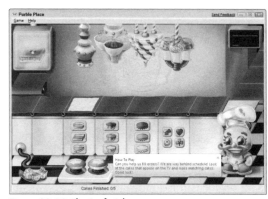

Figure 20-10: The Comfy Cakes game

Play Hearts

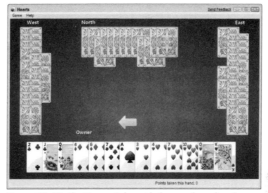

1. Choose Start➪Games and double-click Hearts.

2. In the resulting Hearts window, as shown in Figure 20-11, your hand is displayed while others are hidden. Begin play by clicking three cards to pass to your opponent and then clicking the Pass Left button.

3. Each player moving clockwise around the window plays a card of the same suit by clicking it. The one who plays the highest card of the suit in play wins the trick. (A *trick* is the cards you collect when you play the highest card of the suit.)

Figure 20-11: The Hearts window with three cards ready to be passed

4. Choose Game➪Options to change the settings shown in Figure 20-12. You can rename the other three players, play sounds, show tips, or specify how to save a game.

5. To end the game, choose Game➪Exit or click the Close button.

 Check out the menus in the Games window (Start➪Games) for organizing and customizing the various games that Windows 7 makes available and to set Parental Controls.

Figure 20-12: The Hearts Options dialog box

Add a USB Joystick to Your Computer

1. To connect a Universal Serial Bus (USB) joystick or other type of game controller, simply plug it into a USB port on your computer. Connect to a game port by plugging the device into the port you want to use on your computer. Windows should recognize it and install it automatically.

2. If your device isn't recognized automatically, continue with the following steps.

3. Choose Start⇨Games⇨Tools⇨Input Devices.

4. In the resulting Game Controllers dialog box, as shown in Figure 20-13, click Advanced.

5. In the resulting dialog box, click the arrow on the Preferred Device field to display a list of controllers, click the one that you plugged in, and then click OK twice.

 If your device controller isn't listed in the Game Controllers dialog box, insert the installation disc that came with it and follow directions to install it. If you don't have an installation disc, either the device manual or the manufacturer's Web site might indicate that there's a compatible driver that's already installed with Windows that you could use, so follow Step 5 to select that driver. Alternatively, you can click the Custom button, make selections there, and let Windows select a likely driver. One final option: The manufacturer might offer a down-loadable version of the driver on its Web site.

Figure 20-13: The Game Controllers dialog box

Playing Music in Windows 7

*W*ho doesn't love music? It sets our toes tapping and puts a song in our hearts. It's the perfect accompaniment to spice up the drudgery of working on a computer for hours on end, so wouldn't it be great if you could play music right at your desk without having to take up valuable desktop space with a CD player or even an iPod?

Good news: You might not realize it, but your Windows 7 computer is a lean, mean, music machine. With a sound card installed and speakers or headphones attached, it's a hi-tech desktop boombox that can play sound files and CD/DVDs. With Windows media programs, you can create playlists and even burn music tracks to a CD/DVD or sync to your portable device to download music to it.

The ins and outs of music on your computer, which you discover in this chapter, include

➡ Getting your computer ready for listening by setting up your speakers and adjusting the volume.

➡ Playing music with Microsoft Media Player.

➡ Managing your music by creating playlists of tracks you download.

➡ Burning tracks to CD/DVD or syncing with portable music devices.

➡ Making settings to copy music from CD/DVDs to your computer (or *ripping*).

Get ready to . . .

Set Up Speakers

1. Attach speakers to your computer by plugging them into the appropriate connection (often labeled with a little megaphone or speaker symbol) on your CPU, laptop, or monitor.

2. Choose Start⇨Control Panel⇨Hardware and Sound; then click the Manage Audio Devices link (under the Sound category).

3. In the resulting Sound dialog box (see Figure 21-1), click the Speakers item and then click the Properties button.

4. In the resulting Speakers Property dialog box, click the Levels tab, as shown in Figure 21-2, and then use the Speakers slider to adjust the speaker volume. *Note:* If a small red x is on the speaker button, click it to activate the speakers.

5. Click the Balance button. In the resulting Balance dialog box, use the L(eft) and R(ight) sliders to adjust the balance of sounds between the two speakers.

6. Click OK three times to close all the open dialog boxes and save the new settings.

 If you use your computer to make or receive phone calls, check out the Communications tab of the Sound dialog box. Here you can have Windows automatically make adjustments to sounds to minimize background noise.

Figure 21-1: The Sound dialog box

Figure 21-2: The Speakers Properties dialog box, Levels tab

Adjust System Volume

1. Choose Start⇨Control Panel⇨Hardware and Sound.

2. Click the Adjust System Volume link under Audio Devices and Sound Themes to display the Volume Mixer dialog box (as shown in Figure 21-3).

3. Make any of the following settings:

   • Move the Device Volume slider to adjust the main system volume up and down.

   • For sounds played by Windows, adjust the volume by moving the Applications slider.

   • To mute either main or application volume, click the speaker icon beneath either slider so that a red x appears.

4. Click the Close button twice.

 Here's a handy shortcut for quickly adjusting the volume of your default sound device. Click the Volume button (which looks like a little gray speaker) in the system tray. To adjust the volume, use the slider on the Volume pop-up that appears, or select the Mute check box to turn off sounds temporarily.

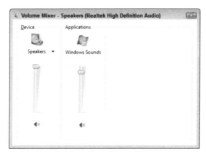

Figure 21-3: The Volume Mixer dialog box

 Today many keyboards include volume controls and a mute button to control sounds from your computer. Some even include buttons to play, pause, and stop audio playback. Having these buttons and other controls at your fingertips can be worth a little extra in the price of your keyboard.

Create a Playlist

1. Choose Start⇨All Programs⇨Windows Media Player.

2. Click the Library button. A blank playlist appears in the Play pane on the right.

3. Click a category (for example, Music) to display libraries, and then double-click a library in the left pane; the library contents appear (see Figure 21-4). Click an item and then drag it to the new playlist. Repeat this step to locate additional titles to add to the playlist.

4. When you finish adding titles, click Save List. To play a playlist, click it in the Library pane and then click the Play button.

5. You can organize playlists by clicking the Organize button (see Figure 21-5) and then choosing Sort By. In the submenu that appears, sort by features, such as title, artist, or release date.

 You can also right-click a playlist in the Library pane and choose Play to play it or choose Delete to delete the list, though the original tracks that make up the list still exist.

Figure 21-4: Building a playlist in the Play pane

Figure 21-5: The Organize menu

Burn Music to a CD/DVD

1. Open the Windows Media Player and then insert a blank CD or DVD suitable for storing audio files in your computer CD/DVD-RW drive.

2. Click the Burn tab, and then click one or more albums or playlists to play and drag them to the Burn pane (see Figure 21-6).

3. Click Start Burn. Windows Media Player begins to burn the items to the disc. The Status column for the first song title reads `Writing to Disc` and changes to `Complete` when the track is copied.

4. When the burn is complete, your disc is ejected (although you can change this option by clicking the Burn Options button and choosing Eject Disc after Burning to deselect it).

 If you swap music online through various music-sharing services and then copy them to CD/DVD and pass them around to your friends, always do a virus check on the files before handing them off. Also, be sure you have the legal right to download and swap that music with others.

Figure 21-6: Music displayed in the Burn pane waiting to be copied

 Note that DVDs come in different types, including DVD+, DVD– and DVD+/–. You must be sure your DVD drive is compatible with the disc type you're using, or you can't burn the DVD successfully. Check the packaging for the format before you buy!

Sync with a Music Device

1. Connect a device, such as an iPod, to your computer and open Windows Media Player.

2. Click the Sync tab; a Device Setup dialog box appears (see Figure 21-7).

3. Name the device, and click Finish. The device is now synced with Windows Media Player and will be automatically updated whenever you connect it to your computer.

 To add items to be synced to a device, with the Sync tab displayed, simply drag items to the right pane. If you're connected, or the next time you connect, the items are copied onto the device automatically.

 If you want to be sure that the sync is progressing, click the Sync Options button (it's on the far right of the top of the Sync tab and looks like a little box with a check mark in it) and choose View Sync Status.

Figure 21-7: The Device Setup dialog box

Play Music

1. Choose Start⇨All Programs⇨Windows Media Player.

2. Click the Library tab and then double-click Music or Playlists to display a library like the one shown in Figure 21-8. Click an album or playlist to open it; the titles of the songs are displayed in the right pane.

3. Use the buttons on the bottom of the Player window (as shown in Figure 21-9) to do the following:

   • Click a track and then click the Play button to play it.

   • Click the Stop button to stop playback.

   • Click the Next or Previous buttons to move to the next or previous track in an album or playlist.

   • Use the Mute and Volume controls to pump the sound up or down without having to modify the Windows volume settings.

 Tired of the order in which your tracks play? You can use List Options button on the Play Pane and chose Shuffle List to have Windows Media Player move around the tracks on your album randomly. Click this button again to turn off the shuffle feature.

 To jump to another track, rather than using the Next and Previous buttons, you can double-click a track in the track list in the Media Player window. This can be much quicker if you want to jump several tracks ahead or behind of the currently playing track.

Figure 21-8: A selected album or playlist

Figure 21-9: The playback tools

Make Settings for Ripping Music

1. If you place a CD/DVD in your disc drive, Windows Media Player asks whether you want to *rip* the music from the disc to your computer. Doing so stores all the tracks on your computer. To control how ripping works with Windows Media Player, click the Organize button and choose Options.

2. Click the Rip Music tab to display it.

3. In the resulting window (see Figure 21-10), you can make the following settings:

   • Click the Change button to change the location where ripped music is stored; the default location is your Music folder.

   • Click the File Name button to choose the information to include in the filenames for music that's ripped to your computer (see Figure 21-11).

   • Choose the audio format to use by clicking the Format drop-down list.

   • Many audio files are copyright protected. If you have permission to copy and distribute the music, you might not want to choose the Copy Protect Music check box; however, if you're downloading music you paid for and therefore should not give away copies of, you should ethically choose to Copy Protect music so that Windows prompts you to download media rights or purchase another copy of the music when you copy it to another location.

   • If you don't want to be prompted to rip music from CD/DVDs you insert in your drive, click the Rip CD Automatically check box.

4. When you finish making settings, click the OK button.

Figure 21-10: The Options dialog box, Rip Music tab

Figure 21-11: The File Name Options dialog box

Working with Photos

A picture is worth a thousand words, and that's probably why everybody is in on the digital image craze. Most people today have access to a digital camera (even if only on their cellphones) and have started manipulating and swapping photos like crazy, both online and off.

Although Chapter 4 gives you a quick peek at how to view images in the Photo Viewer, in this chapter you go a little further. Here you discover how to

➡ View your photos and add tags and ratings to help you organize and search through photos.

➡ E-mail a photo to others or burn photos to a CD or DVD to pass around to your friends.

➡ Create and view a slide show with Windows Explorer Pictures Library.

Chapter 22

Get ready to . . .

View a Digital Image in the Windows Photo Viewer

1. Right-click the Start button and choose Open Windows Explorer.

2. In the resulting window, double-click the Pictures Library icon. If folders are in this library, double-click one. Double-click any photo in the Pictures Library folder. In the Windows Photo Viewer window, as shown in Figure 22-1, you can use the tools at the bottom (see Figure 22-2) to do any of the following:

   • The Next and Previous icons move to a previous or following image in the same folder.

   • The Display Size icon in the shape of a magnifying glass displays a slider you can click and drag to change the size of the image thumbnails.

   • The Delete button deletes the selected image.

   • The Rotate Clockwise and Rotate Counterclockwise icons spin the image 90 degrees at a time.

   • The center Play Slide Show button with a slide image on it displays the images in your Pictures folder in a continuous slide show.

 If you want to quickly open a photo in another application, click the Open button at the top of the Windows Photo Viewer window and choose a program, such as Paint or Microsoft Office Picture Manager.

Figure 22-1: The Windows Photo Viewer window

Figure 22-2: The tools you can use to manipulate images

Add a Tag to a Photo

1. To create a new tag, choose Start⇨Pictures. Right-click a photo and choose Properties.

2. In the Properties dialog box that appears, click the Details tab (see Figure 22-3).

3. Click the Tags item, and a field appears. Enter a tag(s) in the field (see Figure 22-4) and click OK to save the tag.

4. Now if you display your Pictures Library in Windows Explorer in Details view, the tag will be listed next to the photo. Tags are also used when you view photos in Windows Media Center.

 To delete a tag, just display the photo Properties dialog box again, click to the right of the tag, and press Backspace.

 To see a list of all photos in Windows Explorer organized by tags, click the arrow on the Arrange By item and choose Tag.

Figure 22-3: A photo Properties dialog box, Details tab

Figure 22-4: Adding a tag to a photo

Add or Change a Photo Rating

1. To change the rating for a photo so you can arrange your photos by that rating in the Pictures Library, choose Start⇔Pictures. Right-click a photo and choose Properties.

2. In the Properties dialog box that appears, click the Details tab.

3. Click the star that represents the rating you want, from 1 to 5 (see Figure 22-5), and then click OK to save the rating. You can now view the rating in the Pictures Library in Detail view.

   You can rate photos by whatever criteria you want. For example, most liked to least liked, higher quality to lower quality, or you can use a rating to remind yourself that you don't have rights to use certain photos in published documents.

Figure 22-5: Rating a photo in the Properties dialog box

E-Mail a Photo

1. Choose Start➪Pictures. In the Pictures Library, as shown in Figure 22-6, click a thumbnail to select the photo. To choose multiple photos, hold down the Ctrl key and click additional thumbnails.

2. Right-click on the selected files and choose Send To➪ Mail Recipient. In the Attach Files dialog box that appears (see Figure 22-7), change the photo size by clicking the Picture Size drop-down arrow and choosing another size from the list if you wish.

3. Click Attach. An e-mail form from your default e-mail appears with your photo attached.

4. Fill out the e-mail form with an addressee, subject, and message (if you wish), and then click Send.

 Choose smaller size photos to attach to an e-mail because graphic files can be rather big. You might encounter problems sending larger files, or others might have trouble receiving them. Using a smaller size is especially important if you're sending multiple images. *Note:* Although you can send a video file as an e-mail attachment, you can't resize it; video files make photo files look tiny by comparison, so it's probably better to send one at a time, if at all.

 You can also open an e-mail form first. Then, with the Photo Viewer open, click and drag a photo to your e-mail. This method attaches the original file size to the message.

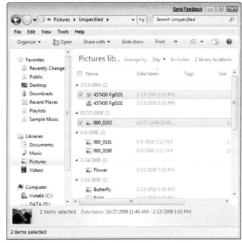

Figure 22-6: Picture files selected in Pictures Library

Figure 22-7: The Attach Files dialog box

Burn a Photo to a CD or DVD

1. Insert a writable CD or DVD disc into your disc drive.

2. With the Pictures Library open in Windows Explorer, display a photo by locating it with the navigation pane and double-clicking the thumbnail to display it in Windows Photo Viewer.

3. Click the Burn button and then choose Video DVD.

4. In the resulting Windows DVD Maker dialog box (see Figure 22-8), click the Add Items button if you want to burn additional photos to the DVD. Locate another photo and then click Add in the dialog box that appears and repeat this procedure until all the photos have been added.

5. Enter a name in the DVD Title field at the bottom of the Windows DVD Maker window (the default name is today's date) and then click Next.

6. In the Ready to Burn DVD window that appears (see Figure 22-9), click the Burn button to proceed.

7. When the files have been burned to the disc, a confirming dialog box appears, and your disc drawer opens. Click Finish to complete the process and close Windows DVD Maker.

 If you want to check the photos you've added before you burn the DVD, click the Preview button in the Ready to Burn DVD window.

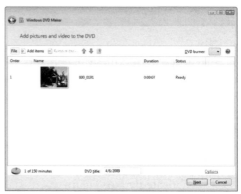

Figure 22-8: The first Windows DVD Maker dialog box

Figure 22-9: Images ready to be burned to a disc

Create and Play a Slide Show

1. Choose Start⇨Pictures. Double-click the Pictures Library folder to display all the pictures within it.

2. Click the check box next to an image to select it. Repeat this to select all the photos you want to appear in the slide show (see Figure 22-10).

3. Click the Slide Show button. The first image appears in a separate full screen display (click Alt+Tab to go to this display). The slides move forward automatically, cycling among the photos repeatedly (see Figure 22-11).

4. Press Esc to stop the slide show.

 If you want a more sophisticated slide show feature, check out Windows Media Center. Here you can create and save any number of custom slide shows, reorganize slides, and edit slide shows to add or delete photos. You might also consider a commercial slide show program, such as PowerPoint, if you want to create more complex slide shows.

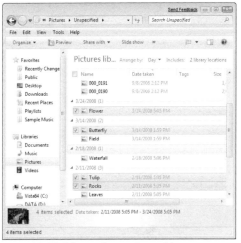

Figure 22-10: Selecting photos in Pictures Library

Figure 22-11: A full-screen slide show display

Index

• S •